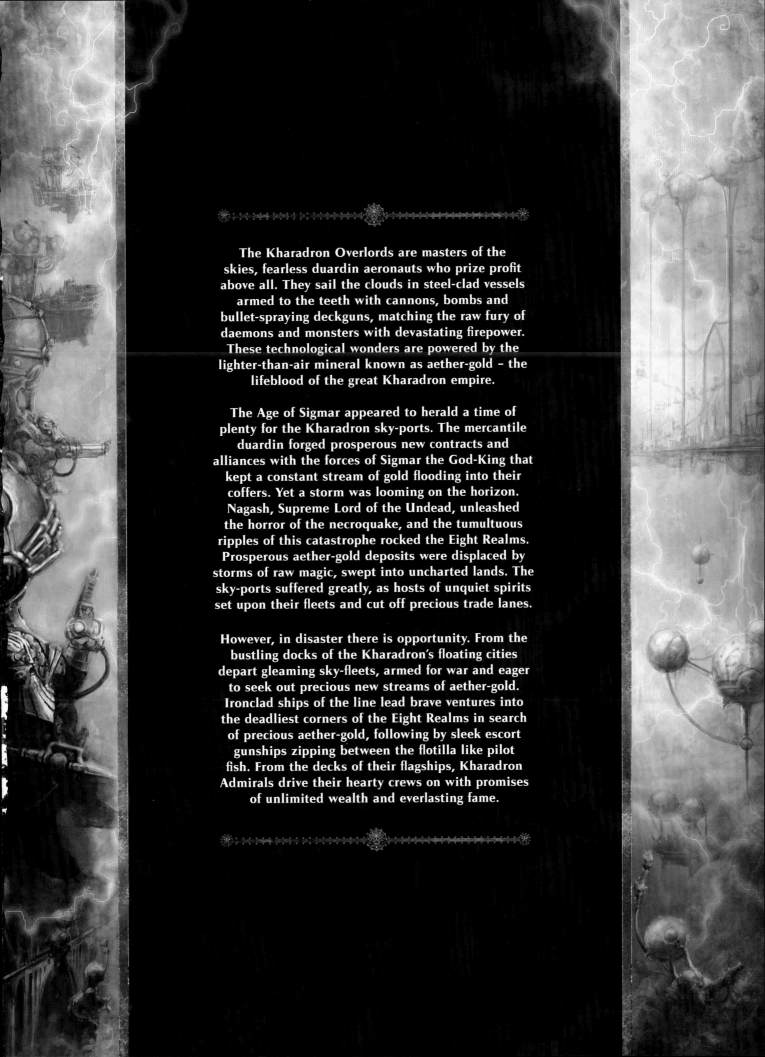

The Kharadron Overlords are masters of the skies, fearless duardin aeronauts who prize profit above all. They sail the clouds in steel-clad vessels armed to the teeth with cannons, bombs and bullet-spraying deckguns, matching the raw fury of daemons and monsters with devastating firepower. These technological wonders are powered by the lighter-than-air mineral known as aether-gold – the lifeblood of the great Kharadron empire.

The Age of Sigmar appeared to herald a time of plenty for the Kharadron sky-ports. The mercantile duardin forged prosperous new contracts and alliances with the forces of Sigmar the God-King that kept a constant stream of gold flooding into their coffers. Yet a storm was looming on the horizon. Nagash, Supreme Lord of the Undead, unleashed the horror of the necroquake, and the tumultuous ripples of this catastrophe rocked the Eight Realms. Prosperous aether-gold deposits were displaced by storms of raw magic, swept into uncharted lands. The sky-ports suffered greatly, as hosts of unquiet spirits set upon their fleets and cut off precious trade lanes.

However, in disaster there is opportunity. From the bustling docks of the Kharadron's floating cities depart gleaming sky-fleets, armed for war and eager to seek out precious new streams of aether-gold. Ironclad ships of the line lead brave ventures into the deadliest corners of the Eight Realms in search of precious aether-gold, following by sleek escort gunships zipping between the flotilla like pilot fish. From the decks of their flagships, Kharadron Admirals drive their hearty crews on with promises of unlimited wealth and everlasting fame.

CONTENTS

PRODUCED BY THE WARHAMMER STUDIO
With thanks to The Faithful for their additional playtesting services.

Games Workshop Ltd., Willow Road, Lenton, Nottingham, NG7 2WS, United Kingdom
games-workshop.com

Led by the renowned Lord-Magnate Brokk Grungsson, an airfleet out of Barak-Nar descends from the clouds intent on securing a mighty haul of aether-gold for its sky-port.

MASTERS OF THE SKIES

High above the clouds of the Mortal Realms there thrives an empire of unrivalled prosperity and aerial power. Guided by the wisdom of their Code, the Kharadron Overlords send forth airship fleets to dominate the skyways – all who challenge the Kharadron's supremacy are quick to suffer the wrath of their techno-arcane war machines.

Bursting from the clouds on contrails of vapour come squadrons of broad-framed airships, their aethercannons swivelling to bear upon grounded foes before opening fire with the fury of a volcanic eruption. Nimble escort ships dart between the hulls of flying fortresses, well-drilled gunners adding their own withering volleys to the barrage. The sheer devastation unleashed by this considerable arsenal turns the world to fire and smoke. Whatever is left of the Kharadron's enemies stagger from the inferno in time to see the airships descend, spilling battle-hardened crews of privateers into the fray. Grizzled duardin sky-dogs leap over the gunwales with cutlasses drawn and shanties upon their lips, eager to earn both glory and a fine haul of plunder.

MERCANTILE MASTERS

The Kharadron Overlords are a conglomerate of duardin powers united by a shared legacy of sky travel and a burning desire for the miraculous resource known as aether-gold, which powers their empire. Unlike the majority of their duardin kin, the Kharadron long ago forsook their ancient mountain holds, and took to the clouds upon floating cities known as sky-ports. There, they survived the devastation of the Age of Chaos, cleaving to the document known as the Kharadron Code – an exhaustive set of guidelines, laws and transactional rules that governs the often messy business of commerce and dictates the Overlords' every decision.

For centuries the Kharadron dwelt in isolation, trading amongst themselves as their airfleets repelled endless assaults from the daemonic servants of the Dark Gods. When Sigmar the God-King returned to the realms at the dawn of a new age, driving back the Chaos hordes and erecting proud free cities amidst the wilds of the realms, the Kharadron sensed great opportunity. They

ended their isolation, setting their devastating aerial firepower against the enemies of civilisation, and striking oaths of alliance with the armies of the heavens. In Sigmar's rising empire, the Kharadron saw a lucrative new trading partner, and ever since their return, duardin airships laden with rare and exotic goods have become a common sight in the docklands of many free cities.

Short and stocky, Kharadron are comparable in stature to their ground-dwelling kin, and possess many similar traits; they are stubborn, resilient as stone, and take great pride in hard work and iron discipline. However, there are also marked differences. For one, the Kharadron largely scorn organised worship, save for the more traditionalist sky-ports such as Barak-Thryng. Kharadron acknowledge the presence of magic and godly beings of course, but they believe that there is a rational, science-based formula behind all outwardly inexplicable happenings.

Kharadron society is well ordered and highly meritocratic. Each of the sky-ports is governed by an Admirals Council, which in turn presides over a body of the six most powerful guilds in that city. Every single captain, guild, company and council member is considered for

their position due to a combination of their innate talent, professional record and potential for increasing their sky-port's profits. The bottom line is all that matters.

The image of Grungni – the duardin smith-god – adorns many Kharadron vessels and statues, though to the majority of these duardin he is more a sign of fortune and a paternal ancestor-spirit than a figure of active worship in their lives. If the tribulations of the Age of Chaos taught the Kharadron Overlords anything, it was that they must rely on their own ingenuity and fortitude, and not upon the benevolence of far-off deities.

Pragmatism also governs the Kharadron's approach to matters of honour. While they take sworn oaths as seriously as any duardin, the Kharadron are perfectly willing to exploit loopholes and technicalities in loosely worded contracts to maximise their advantage – and material gain – in any situation. 'Never sign a Kharadron writ without reading it ten thousand times' is a common saying amongst Dispossessed clan-chiefs, and it is wise advice; though the sky-duardin are not callous beings, they display a notoriously flexible moral compass when it comes to matters of business. As far as they are concerned, anyone foolish enough to sign a contract without fully anticipating any and all potential outcomes deserves no sympathy whatsoever.

This mercenary attitude has caused a deal of friction between the Kharadron and representatives of the free cities, but by and large the relationship between the sky-ports and their Sigmarite allies is cordial; both benefit greatly from the other's presence, and rely on their support in times of war. That said, Kharadron look upon foreigners as somewhat naive and uneducated, and many less scrupulous Captains and Admirals have taken advantage of their neighbours, charging extortionate prices for much-needed supplies, undermining their trading partners whenever possible, and making a killing through the sale of useless gewgaws that they claim possess the power to ward off evil spirits. The nefarious sky-port of Barak–Mhornar has long been suspected of involvement in the illicit trade of cursed artefacts and other forbidden items funnelled through the black markets of the free cities, though its council has been swift to deny these rumours.

'Spectral entities shall not be considered subject to the rules of engagement as dictated in the Third Artycle of the Code.

Additional: no contract of any kind may be agreed with a party that cannot take and hold a draught of kezraak in confirmation of said arrangement.'

kezraak – Kharadron stout

- Amendment Thirty-seven to Artycle Nine of the Kharadron Code, ratified by the Admirals Council in the aftermath of the Shyish necroquake

For all their cut-throat business acumen, the Kharadron seldom risk open war with their trading partners. This is a stance born of cold logic more than anything else, for the Kharadron scorn decisions based on emotion. They remember well the Age of Chaos, when duardin stubbornness and reluctance to accept the inevitable almost led to the destruction of their entire race. The Kharadron also recognise that a realm dominated by the God-King will be a sight more profitable than one conquered by the undead legions of Nagash, smashed to rubble by greenskin hordes, or corrupted by the vile touch of Chaos. When war calls, the sky-ports rally to the side of civilisation – though they always ensure that they receive fitting compensation for their efforts.

AIRPOWER EMPIRE

The Kharadron sky-ports claim dominion over the airways of the Mortal Realms, and there are few who would dispute that assertion. These enormous, floating citadels are both bustling hubs of trade and military strongholds, capable of drifting vast distances in search of prosperous lands and blasting invading armies out of the sky with barrages from their gigantic aethercannon arrays. Visitors from all across the realms are welcomed into the sky-ports' bustling dock-districts and merchant quarters, where every imaginable treasure and exotic resource is available to purchase.

The secret to the sky-duardin's military and economic might is their mastery of aether-gold. This magical substance is found as vapour in the skies of the Mortal Realms and, amongst a thousand other uses, is processed in order to power the Kharadron's mighty ships of the line and their weapons of war. The sky-ports' desire for aether-gold is all consuming, and with every sunrise scores of prospector fleets are despatched in pursuit of valuable new mining territories. Each of these ventures is led by an Admiral, who chooses a single vessel – typically the largest and deadliest in the fleet – as his flagship. Hardened privateers with a keen eye for opportunity, Kharadron Admirals are responsible for ensuring that each voyage culminates in a healthy share of riches for their crew.

From the smallest escort gunship to the mightiest heavy cruiser, these imposing, steel-hulled vessels are built to dominate the skies. When the need arises, they are equally deadly when fighting close to the ground. Each member of a sky-ship's crew is a soldier as much as an aeronaut, rigorously trained for battle and armed with a lethal combination of pistols, boarding axes and cutlasses. When the fleets go to war, the ships of the line can also call upon battle-hardened Grundstok Marines, specialist soldiers hired to repel boarders and obliterate anything that stands between a Kharadron skyvessel and its prize.

In recent times, the prosperity of the sky-ports has been greatly threatened by an outpouring of untapped magic. Nagash – the God of Undeath – inverted the arcane energies of Shyish through a vast necromantic ritual, giving rise to the all-devouring vortex known as the Shyish Nadir. The creation of this black abyss at the heart of the Realm of Death sent a shockwave across reality, throwing the laws of magic into disarray. Storms of gheists were dragged up from the underworlds to prey upon the living, and rampaging, predatory spells wrought great destruction on the business interests of the sky-ports.

The Kharadron named this grim event the Garaktormun, or the Great Gale of Death. Its effect on their trading monopolies and mining of precious aether-gold was significant. Such was the aetheric disturbance in the skies that many of the greatest and most lucrative seams were swept wildly off course, dragged far across the realms into uncharted regions. Once reliable revenue streams were thrown into complete disarray, and hundreds of guilds and companies were ruined in a few short months.

Yet as the Kharadron are so fond of saying, adversity is the bedfellow of opportunity. The sudden vacuum caused by the loss of so many established mining zones led to a new age of prospection and exploration, an aether-gold hunt greater and bolder than anything seen since the earliest days of the Kharadron Overlords' mighty empire.

The Kharadron Overlords' military might is founded upon two supreme truths: firstly, that there is no problem that cannot be overcome by duardin technology; and secondly, that no foe can stand for long in the face of unrelenting and utterly overwhelming firepower. Both doctrines have proven formidably effective.

RISE OF THE OVERLORDS

The Kharadron Overlords' hard-nosed pragmatism is a remnant of their empire's traumatic birth. In order to survive the horrors of the Age of Chaos, many duardin mountain kingdoms were forced to abandon their ancient culture and forge a new path. It is a measure of their resolve and ingenuity that they succeeded.

The origins of the Kharadron Overlords' mercantile empire lie in strife and bloodshed. In ages past the progenitors of the sky-duardin dwelt in Chamon, Realm of Metal. Great portions of this strange, alchemical realm had been fashioned by the smith-god Grungni into perfectly geometric continents, their ferric crusts and mountain ranges filled with all manner of priceless resources – including the rare realmstone Chamonite, a quicksilver-like liquid metal that could be used to power the most wondrous machinery. Having crafted these perfectly ordered lands for his children, Grungni departed for Azyr, the Realm of Heavens, to fulfil an ancient promise to the God-King Sigmar. The smith-god was not one to coddle his worshippers

and believed that only by thriving without his guiding presence could they grow strong.

For a time, the clans of duardin, men and gholemkind that dwelt in the heartlands of Chamon did indeed thrive. They rampantly drained the resources of the region, using techno-arcane methods to raise gleaming empires of metal that dominated the lands. The great duardin clans were perhaps the most respected of all, dwelling within their wondrous mountain cities and digging deep into the bedrock of Chamon to excavate precious minerals and gems. Yet this age of prosperity and wonder would not last, for the primordial enemies of all mortals were stirring once more. The Chaos God Tzeentch had set his

eyes upon the Realm of Metal, for it blazed with potential and sorcerous energy. In the avarice and desire for power that marked the greatest empires of Chamon, the Changer of the Ways found familiar weaknesses on which to prey. Even as his greater daemons whispered promises into the ears of duardin clan-chiefs and human ferromages, the Lord of Sorcery set in motion the corruption of the Realm of Metal itself. He lured forth the godbeast known as the lode-griffon from the aetheric void, so that it settled at the centre of Chamon. The immense magnetic energies of this mythical avian behemoth twisted and bent the land, and played havoc with the industry of the great clans and kingdoms nearby. In desperation, they sought to slay the lode-griffon with a spell

of transmutation that would turn its form to solid gold. Yet though it was seen through to completion, this ritual was twisted by the hand of one of the Gaunt Summoners – powerful daemonic wizards in thrall to Tzeentch. As the lode-griffon's flesh was turned to metal, its screams tore open a portal at the centre of the Spiral Crux, and the daemons of Tzeentch poured through.

Utterly unprepared for the sheer scale of this sudden invasion, the civilisations of Chamon were overwhelmed. Many proud duardin empires that had thrived for centuries were doomed to a drawn-out fate, sealed within the tombs of their mountain fastnesses to starve or be overrun by the seemingly endless tide of daemons. Yet for a few resolute clans, duardin ingenuity provided one last, desperate hope for survival. The steamhead pioneers, masters of aethermatic extraction and cogwork locomotion, laboured day and night to create the means of their escape.

Utilising advanced sciences bolstered by the wondrous magical substance known as aether-gold, the pioneers raised several cities upon great endrinspheres and aethermatic energisers, escaping the madness engulfing the land by retreating into the skies. These disparate, airborne kingdoms banded together as a loose coalition for mutual protection. Those daemons capable of flight pursued, of course, but the duardin strongholds – that would soon come to be known as sky-ports – had prepared for this; their Gyrocopter pilots fought a tireless battle to clear the clouds, engaging malformed, winged monsters in brutal aerial dogfights. These long years of retreat were unimaginably harsh. Yet in adversity was formed the foundation of a formidable air power.

It was precious aether-gold that offered the ancestors of the Kharadron salvation. This rare, gaseous substance laced the skies of the Realm of Metal. Whenever the sky-ports came across seams of the stuff, they drained them dry, innovating ever swifter and more efficient methods of extraction.

Yet the frantic competition for resources soon caused old rivalries to flare and buried grudges to come to the surface, as each of the sky-ports sought to gather as much aether-gold as possible in order to safeguard their own future at the expense of their rivals. Despite the ever-present threat of Chaos on the horizon, a civil war between these competing air powers seemed inevitable.

THE CODE
In a final attempt to avert disaster, the leaders of the sky-ports agreed to meet in council. The Conference of Madralta – named after the floating island upon which it took place – would last for many days, as the fleets of no less than seven sky-ports levelled their sky cannon batteries at one another overhead. It was no peaceful debate. More than once, violence threatened to break out at the peace table. Yet in the end, the imminent doom of their way of life forced the duardin leaders to compromise, and attempt to set down a series of laws that would allow all to prosper. None wished to repeat the mistakes of the past.

The age-old royal dynasties had failed, in the end, to protect their people. There would be no more kings or queens, nor would the sky-duardin ever again look for divine intervention to save them – they had witnessed the fate of those who relied upon the aid of Grungni, Grimnir and Sigmar when Chaos descended upon them. This new empire would be powered by technology and science rather than faith, and governed by elected leaders chosen for their talent, not the provenance of their blood.

Thus was the first draft of the Kharadron Code laid down. All of the developing sky-ports contributed to this document, which codified the principles of discipline, individual freedom, personal profit and communal security that would become the foundation of the Kharadron Overlords' sky-spanning empire. The word Kharadron itself means something akin to 'born from the sundered mountain' in ancient duardin – although the people of the sky-ports would come to embrace a new culture, they would never forget the trauma that had birthed their great civilisation.

'It was not the gods that saved us. It was not even our skyvessels, nor the thunder of our guns. It was compromise. It was negotiation. It was a transaction between equal parties. The Code saved us, and made us what we are.'

- Grand Admiral Varsk Huninger of Barak-Urbaz

The initial guidelines inscribed in the Kharadron's exhaustive manifesto were taken from naval laws originally intended to maintain discipline aboard a sky-ship. The Code simply took these artcles and expanded upon them to cover the governance of their entire society. The Code stipulates everything, from how aether-gold deposits can be claimed to the rules for engaging foes. The original document included nine artcles, each subdivided into many sections. Therein could be found the Artycles of Union, the Seven Rules of Prosperity and the Twelve Points of Election. Over time there have been amendments to the Code – especially in the aftermath of Nagash's necroquake – although some sky-ports refute them, most notably the ultra-traditionalist Barak-Thryng. Even upon agreed artcles, there is often room for interpretation, and some Captains, particular those hailing from the roguish Barak-Mhornar, are remarkably agile in their ability to navigate the framework of the Code.

THE CODE AMENDED

The constitution of the Kharadron is not set in stone, and can be amended should the Geldraad high council deem it necessary; in the wake of the Garaktormun, no less than seventeen fresh amendments were passed after lengthy, often furious debate.

BARSA HERELSDOTTR

BARAK-NAR

ARTYCLE 1 - THE RULES OF GOVERNANCE, POINT 7

The title of Lord-Magnate is given to any whose profit-reaping brings them into the top ten per cent of earners within the last wind cycle. The Lords-Magnate are afforded first choice of fleets and will be amongst those considered to replace any fallen, deceased or incapacitated members of the Admirals Council.

AMENDMENT 12

In the event that the Admirals Council cannot come to a majority consensus regarding matters of commerce (as defined in Artycles 2 and 7 of the Code), then the Lord-Magnate with the largest contribution in aether-gold shares over the last wind cycle shall provide the deciding vote.

Amendment proposed by Admiral Barsa Herelsdottr of Barak-Nar

ARTYCLE 6 - THE RULES OF THE HIGH AIRS, POINT 2

On the high airs a vessel from any sky-port may seize airships deemed to be a pirate craft or taken by piracy and arrest the persons and confiscate all property on board. The Admirals Court of the sky-port which carried out the seizure may decide upon the penalties to be imposed. If the suspect vessel refuses to adhere to the rule of law and surrender its cargo for inspection, the use of lethal force is acceptable in order to encourage compliance.

AMENDMENT 10, FOOTNOTE 13

An Arkanaut Captain or Admiral has the right to recover salvage from the wreckage of any vessel destroyed upon the aether-tides of the Garaktormun. This shall not be considered an act of piracy as defined by Artycle 6, and all material recovered shall be considered the property of the recovering crew.

Amendment proposed by Grand Admiral Hester Grummund of Barak-Zilfin

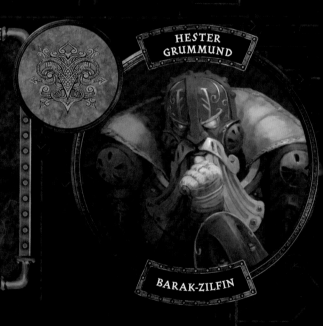

HESTER GRUMMUND

BARAK-ZILFIN

DUGGRUN KHRUNG

BARAK-URBAZ

ARTYCLE 2 - THE 7 RULES OF PROSPERITY, SUB-CLAUSE 12

During an active state of war immediate sanctions shall be imposed upon the enemies of the Kharadron Overlords, the severity of which is to be decided by the Geldraad. As long as the enemy draws breath, they shall be subject to a total trade embargo, and any officer of the fleet who attempts to open negotiations with such a party shall be considered guilty of the highest treason and punished accordingly.

AMENDMENT 3, FOOTNOTE 16

Representatives of the uzkulrik clearly cannot be considered subject to the second stipulation of Sub-clause 12 of Artycle 2, as they do not breathe.

uzkulrik - literally 'bone kings', a Kharadron term for the Ossiarch Bonereapers

Amendment proposed by Admiral Duggrun Khrung of Barak-Urbaz

ARTYCLE 8 - TENETS OF DEFENCE, SECTION 3

Each wind cycle a Musterpress shall be held upon the Brynruf. This shall consist of six days of physical competition and rigorous examinations, the nature of which shall be decided individually by each sky-port's Admirals Council. Upon the culmination of the Musterpress, Admirals and Captains of the fleets shall have seven days in which to offer contracts of service to the contestants.

SUB-AMENDMENT 3F

In times of crisis – as decreed by the Geldraad – representatives from the Grundstok Corporation shall have first option upon all candidates chosen by Musterpress, and shall be allowed to buy out the contract of any Arkanaut at seven twelfths of its set price.

Sub-amendment proposed by Grundstok Marshal Ragnar Kling-Harald of Barak-Zon

RAGNAR KLING-HARALD

BARAK-ZON

MAGBETH IZRUM

BARAK-MHORNAR

ARTYCLE 3 - THE ARTYCLES OF JUSTICE, POINT 5

All hazkal brewed within a sky-port is subject to regular inspection, to be carried out by the Board of Brewmasters. Any guild-company found guilty of thinning their product with bilgewater, using inferior hops or failing to allow appropriate fermentation time shall be fined to the full extent that the Code permits, and its owners de-bearded and branded with the mark of the guzungrim.

hazkal - a strong duardin ale, brewed and fermented over the course of many wind cycles

AMENDMENT 21, FOOTNOTE 6

Brewing stations located within the high airs cannot be subject to point five of this artycle. In addition, the sale of inferior hazkal within foreign ports shall be permitted, because the umgi are content to drink any old swill.

Amendment proposed by Captain Magbeth Izrum of Barak-Mhornar

ARTYCLE 7 - THE RIGHTS OF OWNERSHIP

In order to make a valid claim upon minerals or salvage one must first ensure that the object of said claim is not currently under claim. Newly discovered aether-gold deposits must be marked with angazuben before they can be considered the property of any sky-port. Once a claim is staked, it is illegal to harvest at the site without the owner's permission.

angazuben - aetherically anchored banner-poles left in cardinal directions around a claimed plot

SUB-AMENDMENT 327B

In order to prevent the integrity of the Code against further frivolous and mendacious alterations that undermine the grand tradition of this constitution, no further sub-amendments regarding Artycle 7 shall be brought before the Geldraad.

Sub-amendment proposed by Musterlord Gronki Draug of Barak-Thryng

GRONKI DRAUG

BARAK-THRYNG

THE BREATH OF GRUNGNI

The airborne empire of the Kharadron Overlords relies upon one resource above all others: aether-gold, the sparkling Breath of Grungni. The sky-ports launch fleet after fleet in search of this rare mineral, and are perfectly willing to make war upon their neighbours in order to secure the most prosperous mining fields.

Aether-gold is the lifeblood of Kharadron society. Known as the Breath of Grungni, this lighter-than-air mineral bears the cities of the sky-faring duardin aloft, grants motion to their airships and empowers their weaponry. It is at once the source of the Kharadron Overlords' vast industrial power and their greatest weakness – without precious aether-gold, the duardin's floating empire would quite literally fall from the skies.

Though it can be found across the Eight Realms, aether-gold is not easily mined. In its natural state it is less dense than air, and floats above the cloudline as a sparkling gas or vapour. Not only does the tenuous quality of the metal make it very difficult to locate, but it also means that aether-gold is susceptible to being swept vast distances across the skies by magical storms and other phenomena. Only when refined and processed does aether-gold take on a solid form. In this state it resembles common gold, though its sheen is brighter and it is far stronger and more malleable. The Kharadron –

though cognisant of its miraculous properties – do not think of aether-gold as a magical substance. Instead, they perform all manner of scientific experiments upon it, mixing it with other minerals and subjecting it to a variety of temperatures, conditions and chemicals in an attempt to catalogue the unusual effects that the Breath of Grungni can produce.

The dangers involved in mining aether-gold are manifold. The skies of the Mortal Realms are rarely peaceful, and a sudden magnetic storm or arcane tempest can spell disaster even for a powerful Kharadron ship of the line.

Furthermore, aether-gold seams inevitably draw the attention of magical beasts and predators of the sky – megalofins, harkraken and flocks of blade-feathered rakks – and are of course prized by many rivals of the Kharadron. The change-cults of Tzeentch and the aerial armies of the Grotbag Scuttlers both prize its magical qualities, though thankfully neither of these foes have mastered the processes of refining and weaponising it.

More recently, Cogsmiths of the Ironweld Arsenal have drawn the ire of the sky-ports by attempting to siphon off the substance for their own ends. The Kharadron Overlords do not take threats to their aether-gold monopoly lightly, and are perfectly willing to turn their guns upon rival miners as long as such action can be justified by the Kharadron Code – and there is usually a loophole to be found that allows them to do just that.

Whenever a new vein is discovered, the nearest sky-port is quick to cordon off the area with flotillas of heavily armed Ironclads and Frigates,

AETHER-POWERED ARMS RACE

Kharadron technology is in a constant state of evolution and advancement. In this age of unbound magic, the great guilds have been forced to utilise every iota of their expertise in order to face down new and increasingly terrible threats. The Guilds of the Endrineers and the Aether-Khemists constantly conduct intensive experiments with aether-gold, seeking news ways of weaponising the substance. Recent inventions include incendiary torpedoes capped with slivers of aqthracite, handheld anti-magic repulsors, and aetheric lenses that can gaze through a ship's hull. An entire subdivision of the Endrineers Guild has been tasked with providing the sky-ports with effective countermeasures against the predatory spells that have ravaged many vital trading hubs and exploratory fleets. These methods vary greatly, but Ironclads armed with magic-dampening null projectors and voidstone scatter-mines have proven very effective against hostile tides of magic.

Since the dawn of the necroquake, storms of gheists and wraiths have plagued many of the great sky-ports. Tales abound of lost Barak-Durmmaz, caught in the deathstorms of Shyish and entirely overwhelmed by the spectral processions of the Nighthaunts. It is said that the port still plies the sky-lanes, crewed by the bitter spirits of dead duardin.

In response to similar disasters, many of the sky-ports have decreed the formation of elite Grundstok units specialised in the destruction of 'non-physical entities'. These 'black marines' – so named for the obsidian armour carapaces they wear, regardless of sky-port affiliation – are armed with scatter-shot rifles and equipped with a variety of anti-ethereal equipment and weaponry: celestium burst-grenades, scintillator lenses and aether-vapour projectors. They were first deployed during the Wraith Fleet Conflict, where they fought against the ghostly corsairs of the vampire Varkos Varactyr with notable success.

while specialised dredger-vessels and trawlers began the task of gathering up the bounty. Floating refineries held aloft by endrin-arrays are assembled in particularly prosperous zones, so that the process of extraction and purification can begin without delay. Sometimes, vast territories are entirely devoted to this process. The Goldlanes of the Cathmarn Strait and the Aetherstream of Ziffenbrynyar are sprawling areas dedicated solely to aether-gold harvesting, patrolled by prospector fleets and immense cloud-dredgers.

There is no aspect of Kharadron life that is not driven by the use of aether-gold. Brewery-stations use it to fuel their churning stills. Arkanaut armour is aether-crafted in order to maximise its protective strength while allowing the bearer to move swiftly and surely. Cloud whalers rely on it to power their harpoon cannons, and tavern owners to light up their cramped drinking pits. The Kharadron craft and trade all manner of materials, but even the most mundane creations are – somewhere along the way – reliant upon the transformative power of processed aether-gold.

Such is the Kharadron's desire for more and more of this precious resource that whole reserves can be drained within a matter of weeks, or even days. There are even those Aether-Khemists amongst the more traditional sky-ports, like Barak-Thryng, that fear the avaricious speed with which the fleets are strip-mining the Mortal Realms. What, they ask, would the sky-ports do if the unthinkable happened, and no more seams of aether-gold could be found? Without the means to power their guns and vessels, the Kharadron Overlords would be left at the mercy of their foes. The more prosperous sky-ports such as Barak-Nar and Barak-Zilfin scorn such concerns as laughable pessimism, and with every passing day their consumption of raw resources only gathers pace.

STRIFE AND OPPORTUNITY

The years following the return of the God-King to the Mortal Realms were highly profitable for the sky-ports, as their trading empire grew exponentially with each new city of Order founded. Yet a storm was brewing on the horizon, a maelstrom of magic that would bring about an era of unrivalled change.

The Shyish necroquake – or Garaktormun, as it is known amongst the sky-ports – broke across the domain of the Kharadron Overlords like a crashing wave. In its wake it dragged up tides of gheists from the underworlds, vengeful souls moulded into agents of undeath by the hand of Nagash, the Great Necromancer.

Many other sky-ports soon felt the touch of the grave upon them. Even Barak-Nar, the shining jewel of the Kharadron empire, was not immune. The dockyards of the City of the First Sunrise were all but overwhelmed by Nighthaunt processions, and only a desperate stand by Grundstok Thunderers under the command of the Aether-Khemist Njarn Firewhiskers stopped the tide of gheists from breaching the city proper. The catastrophe caused untold damage, thousands of deaths, and led to over fifty guild-companies filing for bankruptcy. Even greater disasters were occurring elsewhere. Two lesser sky-ports, Barak-Durmmaz and Barak-Kling, were destroyed as the first destructive shockwaves of amethyst magic swept forth from the Realm of Death. Scores of sky-fleets were battered off course, or set upon by howling gales of spectres. The true death toll of those dark days would never be fully accounted for, but estimates from the Endrineers Guild of Barak-Nar alone suggest around one fifth of the sky-port's navy was lost or destroyed in the outbreak of the Garaktormun.

Worse still, the tremendous magical disturbances caused by the necroquake gave rise to sentient spells that ravaged the skies. Purple Suns descended from the clouds, raining cascades of pure death magic that turned everything within reach into unmoving crystal. Snapping jaws of bone materialised in the midst of sky-fleet formations, and in an event that has gone down in infamy, an enormous Aethervoid Pendulum carved the Barak-Zilfin flagship *Sunderer* in twain, the vessel's remains crashing down upon the Hall of Endeavour while the Admirals Council was in session. This caused the deaths of no less than seven of the Windswept City's foremost representatives. To many fighting forces, such losses would be catastrophic, but the Geldraad – the highest ruling council of Kharadron society – swiftly moved to secure new guild-contracts for replacement Ironclad and Frigates, and organise new Musterpresses on a grand scale in order to reinforce the ravaged Arkanaut companies. In addition they ratified several military and societal amendments to the Code, in a reaction to the rapidly changing times.

Such radical action was necessary, for not only did the Shyish necroquake cause great physical damage to the sky-ports, but it also threatened to rob them of their very livelihood. Gaseous deposits of aether-gold were swept vast distances across the realms, carried by the roiling tides of magic. Many of these streams were integral to the sky-ports' profits, and their disappearance was akin to the severing of vital arteries. Yet as befits their adventurous and adaptable nature, the Kharadron Overlords saw opportunity even in these very darkest of hours.

THE GREAT VENTURE

The sky-port councils swiftly realised that the Garaktormun not only brought great danger, but the possibility of securing dramatic new gains. Many of the most prosperous aether-gold streams had long ago been claimed by individual sky-ports, and for decades this monopoly had ensured a familiar hierarchy of influence within Kharadron society. Yet this control had been predicated on those mining routes remaining largely static. Now that so many had been displaced, the intricacies of the Code allowed for new claims to be made by rival powers – so long as they could seek out the missing lodes of aether-gold first. The smell of profit was in the air, and soon the Gorak-drek – the Great Venture – commenced in earnest.

This upheaval would take the Kharadron into new and deadly territories, and see them match their guns against all manner of new foes. Thousands of new voyages were chartered, from scouting missions into hostile lands, to grand expeditions intended to seize vast swathes of territory. The Spiral Crux at the heart of the Realm of Metal saw intense fighting, as Barak-Nar and several other sky-ports converged upon arcane wastes rich with the Breath of Grungni and populated by the servants of Tzeentch – an old enemy who had long contested the Kharadron's dominance of the skies.

So dawned a new age of technological progress and rapid expansion for the Kharadron. Though Barak-Nar maintained the steering hand over the Geldraad, the fortunes of many sky-ports would change drastically, as profits and therefore influence rose and fell dramatically. Some, like Barak-Mhornar, would even take the ultimate risk and depart the Realm of Metal entirely, seeking new and prosperous skies.

THE LANDS BELOW

Although the pursuit of new aether-gold streams is invariably the most pressing issue on the minds of the Geldraad, they have not ceased their attempts to gain a chokehold over trade with their allies in the free cities. Kharadron commercial enclaves in strongholds such as Excelsis, Hammerhal and Greywater Fastness have grown greatly in size and influence, as the sky-ports' merchants flood the markets with rare and wondrous trade goods.

The Kharadron Overlords have a surplus of crude blackpowder weapons and cogwork machines that they happily trade to the inhabitants of Sigmar's cities. These artefacts and engines still have their uses, but they are laughably simplistic compared to the state-of-the-art skyvessels fielded by the sky-ports. The Kharadron look upon the designs of the Ironweld Arsenal and human technologists with something approaching bemused contempt. Less scrupulous Captains been known to take advantage of human naivety by selling bogus tonics, ersatz ale and 'real, genuine realmstone', all at exorbitant prices.

The Stormcast Eternals remain something of an enigma to the Kharadron. The champions of Sigmar's armies do not seem to desire any luxuries, and so most of the Kharadron's entreaties towards them come to naught. Worse still, the archaic, honourbound attitudes of many Stormhosts continue to lead to potentially dangerous misunderstandings. When Admiral Porrbus of Barak-Urbaz attempted to provide a financial incentive for the Knights Excelsior to abandon their defence of the Zephen Skypass and allow Kharadron trading ships access to the rich clouds beyond, the truculent Stormcasts reacted with outrage. An Arkanaut Frigate was downed by Celestar Ballista fire, and the sky-port have since marked the merciless Stormhost as a foe.

Never ones to tie themselves down to a single alliance, the Kharadron Overlords have diversified their trading by making contact with forces outside the influence of Azyr. Deals with the war-obsessed greenskins are – though not unheard of – very rare, but the lords of the deathly Ossiarch Bonereapers have proven quite amenable. Officially the sky-ports are at war with Mortarch Katakros and his soul-constructs, but that has not stopped ivory smugglers out of Barak-Mhornar from making a killing trading bones looted from recent battlefields with the legion known as the Stalliarch Lords. As of late however, these enterprising Admirals have struggled to fulfil the Bonereapers' increasingly outlandish demands – should they fail to do so, the skeletal lords have threatened extreme repercussions.

THE SKY-PORTS

Floating metropolises held aloft by the wondrous power of aether-gold, the Kharadron sky-ports are the dominant power in the skies of the Mortal Realms. Merchants and adventurers flock from afar to visit these technological marvels, for within their bustling dock districts can be found all manner of exotic goods and illicit secrets.

When they first rose from the mountains of Chamon and took to the clouds, the sky-ports of the Kharadron Overlords were floating fortresses, fashioned for survival and armed for war. While they still maintain a formidable array of firepower – as any foe foolish enough to stray within range of their skycannon batteries will attest – they have become much more than mere defensive strongholds. They are amongst the greatest centres of trade in the Mortal Realms, each home to many thousands of duardin and visited by representatives from all of the civilised nations.

The exact size and layout of a sky-port can vary greatly, but the majority are constructed as a series of concentric squares, with the vital administrative and governmental districts placed at the centre. All are bordered by vast and bustling dockyards, which are constant hives of activity. Most sky-ports refuse to allow any non-Kharadron beyond the docklands, and so these quarters are filled to the brim with humans, aelves and other races, whose every desire is catered to by enterprising traders. Bathed in the candescent glow of whaleen-oil lamps, the labyrinthine streets echo to the chattering chorus of a thousand different languages. Endrintrams and steam-gondolas provide access along the canalways that run through the sky-port; these function as sewers and water-pipe routes, but also dispose of waste by spilling it out of hatches to rain down on the lands below.

Above, the skies are choked with airships – not solely military models, but civilian skiffs, bulk haulers and yachts. In the busiest sky-ports, traders can sometimes be forced to wait in lane for several days in order to secure a berth. Barak-Zilfin in particular is known for its heavily congested airlanes. According to the Code, each Sky-port controls all airspace around its domicile within the span of three cannon shots. Beyond that, the expanse of the skies is known as the 'high airs', and is regarded as neutral territory. The borders of each sky-port are guarded by floating fortresses armed with intimidating arrays of cannons and swivel-guns, informally known as 'Zunfar towers', after the Admiral who pioneered their use.

When returning Frigates and their escort vessels make port, troupes of dirty, battle-scarred Arkanauts unload their latest acquisitions before heading deeper into the city to make the most of their temporary leave. Gambling halls, smoke-shrouded darak-dens and garish bawdyhouses all provide much-needed opportunities for Arkanauts to blow off steam. With fresh aether-gold shares burning a hole in their pocket and often only a few days or weeks to make use of, they waste no time getting drunk on cheap ale

and heading to the card tables. This release of pent-up energy sometimes gets a little rough, at which point it is down to the copperhats – a slightly derogatory name for the longshore marshals – to maintain order. These no-nonsense naval police, usually made up of veteran Grundstok Marines injured in the line of duty or neophyte Arkanaut recruits, go about their task methodically with billy clubs and fists.

Beyond the dock districts sprawl endless rows of warehouses, aether-factories and other industrial zones. These sectors are home to the lesser-chartered guilds, and are populated by many thousands of labourers – those duardin who were passed over by the Musterpresses and thus denied a career in the sky-fleets. Despite the Kharadron's undoubted technological mastery, their existence can be a difficult one. Packed together like tinned globfish in almshouses and workhalls, they toil daily for a relative pittance; although Kharadron society is proudly meritocratic, factory bosses have a vested interest in ensuring their downtrodden workers do not rise beyond their station.

While aether-gold can be processed without releasing polluting smoke, much of the Kharadron Overlords' heavy industry utilises other, less refined chemicals and metals. Smog and acidic rain showers are common, despite the use of endrin-bellows and dispersal fans to clear the worst of the contamination. Some sky-ports suffer from this chemical blight more than others; Barak-Nar's relentless industrial drive and Barak-Zon's ever-expanding weapons industries have led to particularly heavy pollution, bringing with it diseases such as sky-miner's consumption, ironscale and the dreaded glowlung. The Aether-Khemists Guild of Barak-Nar has dedicated an entire arm of its alchemical labs to uncovering cures for these epidemics using sub-dermal infusions of aether-gold, but thus far only the richest residents are able to afford such treatment. By contrast, Barak-Thryng's refusal to utilise wasteful, non-traditional methods of generating power means that its skies are relatively clear.

The wealthiest individuals in the sky-port reside close to its thriving heart, in gated towers and floating manses held aloft by a steady flow of aether-gold. From here, the Lord-Magnates and master industrialists of the city quite literally look down upon those less fortunate. Lord-Magnate Kreg Folsson of Barak-Urbaz has constructed an obscenely luxurious endrinvilla right above the refinery in which he once worked as a beardling, so that every day he can see just how far he has come.

At the centre of a sky-port lies its nexus of government, typically located amidst a wondrous plaza district portraying the city's proudest military and economic achievements. These grand old structures include the Hall of Endeavour in Barak-Zilfin, the Sunrise Citadel of Barak-Nar, Barak-Mhornar's mysterious Shadowmark Repository and the Kazakluft of Barak-Thryng. Here the Admirals Council gathers, and the dual businesses of profit and war are debated. No more than a handful of outsiders have ever been granted access to these closely-guarded quarters, but they speak of vast and imposing chambers echoing to the bellicose sounds of Kharadron politics, and populated by minor armies of runescribes and dignitaries.

STRUCTURED FOR PROFIT

From the most minor guild-corporation to the greatest of the sky-ports, all levels of Kharadron society are managed like a business conglomerate. Every decision is governed by the desire for profit, and justified by guidelines laid down in the Kharadron Code.

The free cities of Sigmar have a complex power structure, but even this pales in comparison to the bureaucratic system of governance practised by the Kharadron sky-ports. Overall command of each sky-port goes to the Admirals Council, which is comprised of the most successful officers of the fleet. It is the aim of all Kharadron skyfarers to secure a place on this august body, for they wield incredible power and influence.

Beneath the Admirals Council are the six largest guilds, including the Endrineers Guild, Aether-Khemists Guild and the Fleet Service. The latter is typically the most influential amongst the six, as their airships are vital to the gathering of aether-gold. However, the relative authority of the guilds fluctuates from city to city. Barak-Zilfin, for example, grants great influence to its peerless Nav-League.

Each individual fleet – regardless of size and function – is also subject to its own governing council, whose members act as managing directors. Upon return to port, a Kharadron Admiral answers directly to this board, and they have the right to terminate his contract should he fail to deliver as promised. Furthermore, every single member of the crew is a shareholder with a vested interest in ensuring a successful voyage.

Above even the Admirals Council of each sky-port is the Geldraad, the highest ruling body of Kharadron Overlords society. It is composed of members from the six wealthiest sky-ports, with the number of delegates provided by each determined by capital. Barak-Nar maintains a 'Steering Hand' with six seats, but recent events have caused the fortunes of several great Kharadron powers to rise and fall.

THE STATUS OF WEALTH

	Sky-port	Capital	Delegates
Opposite is a list of the major sky-ports along with their current capital (aether-gold shares) and number of delegates on the Geldraad.	Barak-Nar	296,132,947	6
	Barak-Zilfin	152,753,191	5
	Barak-Mhornar	92,114,885	3
	Barak-Zon	38,653,342	2
	Barak-Urbaz	25,716,102	1
	Barak-Thryng	823,500	1

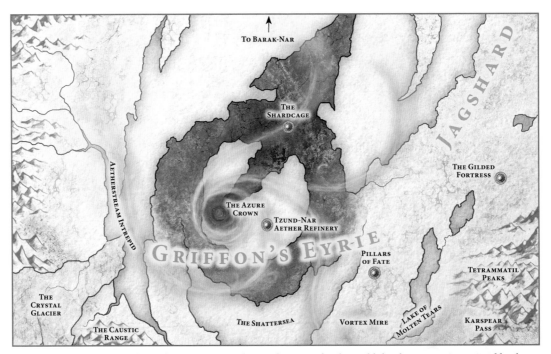

Claimed by Barak-Nar, the Aetherstream Intrepid is a rich source of aether-gold that lies in a region twisted by the influence of Tzeentch. Despite the extreme risks of mining this seam, it has earned the sky-port impressive profits.

THE AETHER-KHEMISTS GUILD

The Aether-Khemists are alchemic scientists. It is with their knowledge that even cloud-obscured aether-gold seams can be located and followed. Indeed, it is only by the genius of their guild's inventions that aether-gold can be siphoned from clouds and refined into a solid substance. The guild trains its members to use a wide range of gadgets, including analytic recogitators, heliotropic distillators and the God's Lung. Their methods are not solely experimental in nature, for an Aether-Khemist must also learn to grade the quality of aether-gold through the only means known – by smell. Aether-Khemists maintain guild centres in all of the sky-ports, but Barak-Urbaz has by far the greatest number, and their members are renowned throughout Kharadron society for their skill at wringing aether-gold from the air.

THE NAV-LEAGUE

The Nav-League is composed of Aetheric Navigators, a secretive order of aerocartographers. It is their lore that has mapped out the troposphere of Chamon and sections of the realm's stratosphere. They study the elements, especially the winds and shifting atmospheric energies. They guide the sky-fleets along aerial trade routes, seeking to catch thermals and avoid the many perils of the airways. Only those that can quickly solve complex mathematical formulas under great duress can hope to pass the entrance exams to attend one of the Navcademies. Yet no matter how rigorous the training, it is nothing compared to hanging onto the deck rails while trying to calculate the shifting currents of the Strahlstrom – just one of the many duties a Navigator is called upon to perform aboard an airship.

THE ENDRINEERS GUILD

The most mechanically inclined Kharadron are apprenticed to the Endrineers Guild. All sky-ports have guild-run Endrineering Academies, the largest of which are the Great Coghalls of Barak-Zilfin. Those who demonstrate skill find profitable employment as artificers, metalcasters, forgekeepers or shipwrights, but only the very best and bravest are sent to work on the Arkanaut fleets themselves. There, they serve the ships as Endrinriggers or, should they survive long enough and accomplish full mech-mastery, as Endrinmasters. The Endrineers Guild is just as protective of its machines as the exacting rites that keep them running, and there is a fair amount of sharp practice between guild members from competing sky-ports, each seeking to undermine or benefit from their rivals' latest innovations.

CHARTERED COMPANIES

Alongside the six major guilds, each sky-port has hundreds of for-profit enterprises known as guild-companies or chartered companies. These organisations make their fortune by selling a particular product or service. The smallest beard-oil sellers or brewsmiths may number only a few scattered depots within their home city, while the largest are incredibly powerful corporate giants that have offices in multiple sky-ports. Iggrind-Kaz Aeronautics, for example, is renowned for the quality of its surge-injection endrins, which utilise liquidised aether-gold to grant a vessel supercharged bursts of speed. The guild-company has depots in five of the six major sky-ports – only Barak-Thryng refuses to allow the upstart company permission sell within its borders, citing improper and wasteful use of the Breath of Grungni.

That has not stopped several Captains native to the sky-port from installing Iggrind-Kaz components in their ships. As the Code allows for guild-companies to trade beyond the borders of their home port, they are often sponsored or partly funded by one of the major guilds, who skim a nice percentage from every bulk sale. The Grundcorps of Barak-Zon, for instance, owns many shares in the weaponsmith Thrund Armoury, whose aethershot rifles are always in high demand for their ruggedness and accuracy. Barak-Thryng's dark ales – brewed according to ancient recipes guarded as fiercely as any military secret – are the envy of all. Guild-companies such as Bugman's Brew and the Grumgar Brothers' Hoppery are in particularly high demand. They even sell their wares in Sigmar's free cities – but only watered-down grog unfit for duardin consumption.

ANNALS OF THE OVERLORDS

With pragmatic ruthlessness and the power of aethermatic technology, the airfleets of the sky-ports have built a vast dominion above the clouds. Here follows a brief history of the Kharadron Overlords and the famous acts of endeavour that helped birth their grand mercantile empire.

⚙ THE AGE OF MYTH ⚙

THE SMITH GOD'S MASTERPIECE

Grungni the Smith God seeks to create a paradise world for his children in the Realm of Metal, Chamon. He constructs a perfectly geometric archipelago at the gleaming centre of the realm and fills it with precious minerals and metals, naming his creation the Godwrought Isles. Clans of humans, duardin and gholemkind all find a home here, growing rich and powerful as they mine the lands. These nascent civilisations include the ancestors of the Kharadron Overlords. Never a deity to coddle his worshippers, Grungni departs to Azyr in order to fulfil an ancient pledge to the God-King, leaving his flock to forge their own destiny.

BREATH OF GRUNGNI

The innovators and inventors known as the steamhead pioneers master the art of extracting aether-gold, a wondrous mineral that swirls about the angular peaks of the Godwrought Isles. They call the stuff the Breath of Grungni, believing it to be the lingering essence of their departed god, and waste no time in discovering ways to refine and process it. It proves a remarkably adaptable substance of near-limitless power, and its properties lead to a new age of scientific progress for the enterprising duardin.

THE SKY-RIFT OPENS

Tzeentch, the Architect of Fate, sets his eyes upon Chamon. Through subterfuge and trickery, he lures the godbeast known as the lode-griffon to the heart of the realm. The creature's terrible magnomantic aura buckles and warps the Godwrought Isles, causing untold death and destruction as the metal land masses are torn apart. Hereafter, this region becomes known as the Spiral Crux. The greatest aethermancers from across the realm seek to slay

the lode-griffon with sorcery and thus bring to an end its malign influence – just as the Change God knew they would. The ritual succeeds and the godbeast is slain, but its death-screams tear apart the fabric of the realms. A great sky-rift opens above the heart of Chamon, spilling Tzeentch's daemonic legions into reality.

⚙ THE AGE OF CHAOS ⚙

ESCAPE TO THE CLOUDS

The Change God's daemon hordes descend upon the great underground kingdoms of the Chamonic duardin, trapping the occupants in their mountain fastnesses. The defenders hold out bravely for many years, but it seems only a matter of time before the hosts of the Chaos Gods breach their walls. Desperate, the normally conservative duardin turn to arcane science and untested machineries in an attempt to save themselves. Combining their nascent mastery of air travel with the aether-gold technologies innovated by the steamhead pioneers, the besieged take to the skies upon weaponised platforms, remaking their fortresses into the first of the sky-ports.

THE GREAT SKY WAR

As the sky-ports rise into the clouds, escorted by squadrons of Gyrocopters and bombers, the armies of the Change God give pursuit. What follows is a desperate flight across the Realm of Metal, with duardin pilots maintaining a ceaseless vigil against the aerial attacks of blade-finned Screamers

and Disc-riding Horrors. The blossoming detonations of scatter-burst torpedoes and cascades of lurid magic ravage the skies, as thousands of duardin aeronauts sell their lives in order to keep the enemy at bay. These immense battles amongst the clouds are only the first engagements of the Great Sky War, a conflict that will rage on for centuries.

THE CONFERENCE OF MADRALTA

Competition between the various sky-ports for precious aether-gold – the only thing that can power their flight across the skies – threatens to lead to all-out war. Upon the floating island of Madralta, fleets from every sky-port hold council. As enemies close in around them, the duardin of the clouds together draft the document known as the Kharadron Code. This will become the foundation of the greatest aerial empire the realms has ever known.

BATTLE OF THE FIRST COALITION

The newly allied Kharadron Overlords are assailed by the infernal fleets of the Tetronomicar, a triad of Tzeentchian Daemon Princes, who have pursued the sky-ports vast distances across the Realm of Metal. Though outnumbered at least two to one, the Kharadron decide to make their stand above the Straits of Helsilver. There, Grand Admiral Horgrumm Brand of Barak-Nar masterminds a famous victory, splitting his fleet into multiple smaller formations in order outmanoeuvre the massive crystal barges of the Trionomicar and blast them into shards one by one. Though Grand Admiral Brand is slain during the thick of the fighting, his forces carry the day, routing the Chaos armada. The engagement ensures the Kharadron Overlords' complete dominance of the Chamonic skies for more than a century and lays down the core tenets of their naval strategy.

CORSAIRS OF THE SHADOW PORT

Mysterious, unmarked vessels begin to prey upon merchant convoys out of Barak-Zilfin and Barak-Nar. After both sky-ports suffer tremendous losses in aether-gold shipments, they discover that the perpetrators are corsairs out of Barak-Mhornar, using rune-markings of illusion to conceal their allegiance. Open war very nearly breaks out; it is only avoided by a series of urgent amendments to the Code prohibiting such fractious behaviour.

● THE AGE OF SIGMAR ●

THE HEAVENS OPEN

Sigmar the God-King sends forth his heavenly armies into the Mortal Realms, seeking to reclaim his ancient lands from the clutches of the Dark Gods. The Stormcast Eternals battle the hordes of Chaos for control of the Realmgates – arcane portals that connect the realms. The Kharadron look on with interest but do not intervene, preferring to hedge their bets before committing to any cause.

VAULT OF THE ELDERS

Seeking to recover priceless relics of its past, an airfleet from Barak-Thryng under the command of Admiral 'Ironbrow' Kreeg commences an excavation of Karak-a-Zaruk, one of the greatest of the duardin strongholds to fall during the Age of Myth. To Kreeg's disgust, he finds that skaven of Clan Moulder have turned the place into an enormous fleshpit for the purposes of creating their hideous abominations. Enraged, the Admiral refuses to leave until every last 'thaggoraki runt' has been blasted into pieces. It is said that Ironbrow has not seen the sky since, as he leads his Grundstok soldiers ever deeper into the karak, wiping out the infestation as he goes.

FEEDING FRENZY

A Barak-Zilfin airfleet commanded by Admiral Kolf Balim is ambushed by an immense armada of Grotbag Scuttlers and suffers heavy losses. In a last, desperate gambit, the Admiral flees through the heart of a megalofin feasting ground. The sky-sharks devour the grots' ramshackle airships by the dozen, but the remnant of Balim's fleet escapes.

TENTATIVE ALLIANCE

In the wake of the climactic battle for the Allpoints, Sigmar begins to construct his free cities in those areas reclaimed from the clutches of the Dark Gods. Identifying a potent new source of trade and income, the Kharadron finally decide to send delegates to the God-King's court.

BATTLE OF VINDICARUM

Vindicarum is assailed by hosts of Chaos daemons, who use an aetheric storm as cover to ambush the Celestial Vindicators standing guard over the city. Though the Stormcasts fight with ferocity, their winged formations of Prosecutors are vastly outnumbered. It is only when the clouds part and an airfleet from Barak-Nar descends upon the daemons with cannons blazing that victory is snatched from the precipice of disaster. In the aftermath of battle, the two victors take steps to secure an alliance. The Treaty of Vindicarum ratifies an economic pact between the sky-ports and the God-King's armies, while a cleverly worded sub-clause ensures that the Kharadron retain sole harvesting rights over the largest seams of aether-gold in Chamon.

BLOCKADE OF BARAK-ZON

The Lord of Change Kairos Fateweaver lays siege to Barak-Zon at the head of a daemonic convocation of Tzeentch. The grizzled defenders of the City of the Sun hold out long enough to be relieved by a confederation of fleets from all the major sky-ports, commanded by Brokk Grungsson. To this day, soldiers of Barak-Zon stubbornly deny that they ever needed saving.

THE GARAKTORMUN

Nagash, the God of Undeath, works a terrible ritual that unleashes a wave of destructive energies across the realms. Not only does the Garaktormun – or 'Great Gale of Death' – give rise to vast numbers of Nighthaunt spirits, but it also sweeps many streams of aether-gold vast distances across the airways.

A NEW INVENTION

Endrineer Drak Grolsson of Barak-Nar invents the aethermatic repulsion field, a device that can keep the sorcerous winds of the Spiral Crux at bay. Other sky-ports fashion their own versions of the device, and it allows the Kharadron to venture into regions long thought inimical to life in search of aether-gold.

THE GRAND TOUR

Lord-Magnate Brokk Grungsson embarks upon a grand tour of Sigmar's free cities and becomes the first Kharadron to meet Sigmar's chief architect Valius Maliti in the industrial stronghold of Greywater Fastness. However, in the wake of this encounter, Grungsson abruptly cancels the rest of his tour and requests a special session of Barak-Nar's Admirals Council. The results of this debate are not made public, but soon afterwards the Barak-Nar trading enclave in Greywater departs, to the great surprise and concern of the city's inhabitants.

BATTLE OF SKRAPPA SPILL

The largest armada ever assembled by Barak-Zon descends upon the greenskin kingdom of Skrappa Spill. The Admirals of the sky-port believe that beneath the junk-mountains of Ayadah lies the *Zangmendrung*, a Kharadron Dreadnought carrying experimental weaponry that was brought down during the Age of Chaos. Squadrons of Frigates swoop down from the ochre clouds of the Spill, pummelling grots and orruks with broadsides as Arkanaut excavation teams leap overboard and into the fray. At first, the battle seems to sway in the Kharadron's favour. The wreckage of the *Zangmendrung* is located, but before the Barak-Zon fleet can fully extract its cargo, the Bad Moon rises above Ayadah and begins to spit loonstone meteors at the airfleet. Several vessels are smashed out of the sky to crash upon the rusty dunes of the Spill. The Barak-Zon armada is forced to retreat with the few artefacts it has recovered. Its Grundstok Thunderers suffer dreadful losses holding the greenskin tide at bay long enough for the survivors of downed vessels to be evacuated.

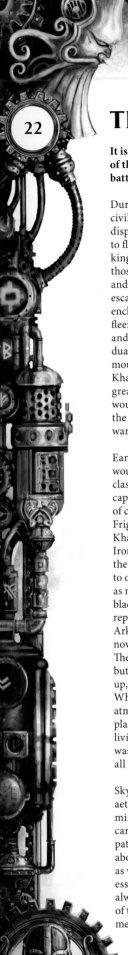

THE ARKANAUT SKY-FLEETS

It is the destructive force of the Kharadron's fearsome airships that ensures their monopoly over the trade lanes of the Mortal Realms and keeps the aether-gold flowing into the coffers of the sky-ports. When an airfleet sails to battle, it carries enough firepower to turn any fortress to smoking rubble.

During the Age of Chaos, civilisations were broken and dispossessed peoples were forced to flee the ruins of their shattered kingdoms. Cast adrift, many of those exiled were slain or captured and pressed into slavery. Those that escaped did so by finding hidden enclaves or living as nomads, forever fleeing to stay ahead of enemy armies and monstrous ravagers. When the duardin were driven out of their mountain holds, the forebears of the Kharadron took to the clouds. Their greatest weapons in the wars to come would be their skyvessels, perhaps the most technologically advanced war machines in the Mortal Realms.

Early designs evolved into what would later become the Arkanaut class of airship. Armour-plated, and capable of carrying a complement of crew and warriors, the Arkanaut Frigate became the mainstay of the Kharadron fleets, with the larger Ironclads serving as flagships. Since the earliest days the duardin learned to outfit their skyborne ships with as much weaponry as possible. The blackpowder weapons of yore were replaced, with the majority of the Arkanauts' impressive arsenals now powered aethermatically. The sky-dwellings that were once but temporary refuges were built up, becoming vast growing cities. When the true riches of the upper atmosphere were discovered, all plans to return to ground-based living were abandoned – and it was the sky-fleets that made it all possible.

Sky-fleets are used to seek out aether-gold and to protect those mining it. The sky-fleets transport cargo, and each sky-port maintains patrol fleets that protect the airspace above and around the floating cities as well as common trade routes. In essence, the sky-fleets are – and have always been – the very lifeblood of the Kharadron Overlords' mercantile empire.

Across each of the different sky-ports, it is the desire of every young beardling to serve aboard the sky-fleets. Competition is fierce amongst the company-sponsored aereonautical academies. There, retired crew and Captains teach – and pass notoriously ruthless judgements upon – their charges, offering ratings to only the most able-bodied. It is in their best interests to do so, of course, for they own stock in the fleets and will be rewarded only if newly crewed ships can return profits.

As the Kharadron Code states, every ship must bear a Captain, a leader who rules the craft absolutely. Whilst aboard, none save the Admiralty have the right to disobey an order. Crews are chosen at the Musterpress and can come from different academies within the same sky-port. Although they hail from different families and backgrounds, once aboard, the crew are bonded by many oaths and Code-prescribed rituals. Crew pride themselves on their loyalty to ship and shipmates, and invariably the most successful sky-fleets employ crew that have served together for decades.

It is possible, as laid out by Artycle 1, Point 5 of the Code, for crew to usurp a captaincy. This is not some riotous act of mutiny, but rather meritocracy at work. Sub-clauses of the Code mandate the replacement of Captains who do not bring success upon a ship, for to rest upon the laurels of past triumphs is not the way of the Kharadron. Captains so deposed are not dishonoured; they merely lose their rank and join the crew, as per Artycle 1, Point 6, where they might rise or fall based on their own achievements like all others.

ORGANISATION OF THE AIRFLEETS

At the top of an airfleet's hierarchy are its commissioned officers. Each airship has a Captain, whose rule over his craft is absolute. When enough ships are grouped together, however, an Admiral is appointed to overall command, and his authority extends further still. Each sky-port has a number of Admirals at its disposal, each with the potential to command an entire airfleet.

The other officers in the fleet hail not from the Arkanaut training academies but are specialists from the guilds – Aetheric Navigators, Aether-Khemists and Endrinmasters. These warrant officers are assigned wherever their skills will serve the sky-fleet best, but they commonly go to war upon its Arkanaut Ironclad. Many fleets boast several such officers. It is especially common for larger flotillas to deploy Endrinmasters equipped with high-speed dirigible suits in order to respond rapidly to mechanical crises across the fleets. Likewise, it is common for prospecting fleets to carry more than one Aether-Khemist, for the more of these alchemical scientists are aboard, the more likely the Kharadron are to sniff out a rich seam of aether-gold.

Arkanaut Frigates and Ironclads are the ships of the line and the mainstay of the fleet, acting as bombers, gunships or transport craft as the Admiral sees fit. An Admiral can pick any ship within the fleet to call his capital ship; this is most often the largest vessel – usually an Ironclad – but sometimes a Frigate of long or distinguished service will have the honour of bearing him to battle. Many Admirals change vessels with each fresh voyage, shrewdly picking a fitting conveyance depending on the requirements of their chartered mission. Others maintain a particular fondness for a single sky-ship, spending the majority of their careers walking the same deck and fighting alongside the same crew. Grundstok Gunhaulers, meanwhile, are hired escort-class fighters, used as interdiction craft or to launch swift assault runs. There have been instances where raids or even large-scale battles have been brought to a successful and profitable conclusion by the use of these ships alone.

The bulk of the sky-fleet's infantry is composed of the Arkanaut Companies, whose primary role is to perform ground-based or boarding actions in furtherance of the fleet's objectives. The more heavily armed and armoured Grundstok Thunderers are professional fighters contracted to safeguard the fleet, though how they perform this duty is often at their discretion. The militaristic sky-port of Barak-Zon often eschews aerial raids entirely in order to deliver elite ground troops into the heart of the enemy position. These combat landings have proven devastatingly effective against fortified positions.

Finally, the Skyriggers are mobile rapid-response specialists whose roles require them to manoeuvre among the other elements of the fleet as the situation demands. Endrinriggers usually enter battle alongside the flagship but will scramble to repair other ships as necessary. The offence-oriented role of Skywardens usually sees them accompany the Grundcorps into battle.

While each sky-port has its own distinct way of organising the different components of its fleets – from the hun-ghrumtok ('heavy bomber wing') of Barak-Thryng to the mighromtok ('scout patrol wing') of Barak-Zilfin – all are assembled from the same core of officers, troops and airships. It is a system that has served the Kharadron well and enforced their dominance of the skies across the Mortal Realms.

HIERARCHY OF THE SKY-LORDS

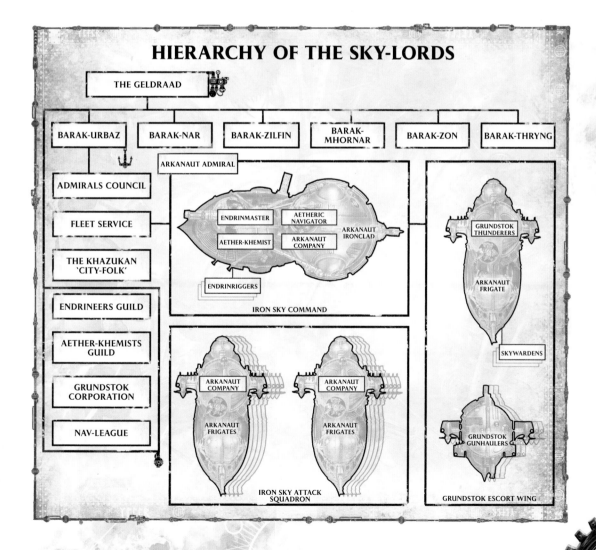

DWELLINGS OF THE KHARADRON

BARAK-URBAZ

It is said that bartering with a trader from Barak-Urbaz is more treacherous than navigating a shoal of stunfish. Barak-Urbaz is the most cosmopolitan sky-port, and its citizens pursue profit with unmatched zeal. This city boasts the greatest sky-fishing fleets, for its Codewrights long ago won Code Claims to several cloudbanks rich in life. Further income pours into the sky-port from Realmgates known only to its Admirals Council, and its fleets ferry people or goods through these portals to any realm for a fee. The most skilled Aether-Khemists come from Barak-Urbaz, and their methods ensure that not even the clouds can avoid being squeezed for profit.

During the Time of Tribulations, many Captains of Barak-Urbaz made a fortune providing safe passage – often at a significantly marked-up price – for citizens of Sigmar's free cities who were fleeing the destruction wrought by Nagash's necroquake. The cynical behaviour of several of these skyfarers led to the infamous Seven-Day War, during which an irate Freeguild General from Hammerhal Aqsha opened fire upon the fleet of Admiral Ubb Kengaz, furious at the unscrupulous Kharadron's apparent abandonment in Chaos-held territory of several thousand passengers who no longer had the coin to pay them.

BARAK-MHORNAR

Labelled pirates or worse by the duardin of the other sky-ports, the denizens of Barak-Mhornar are regarded with no small amount of irony as great innovators when it comes to interpreting the Kharadron Code. Indeed, several of the amendments that have been added to the original document were ratified specifically to halt depredations largely being carried out by privateers from Barak-Mhornar. The guile of those who hail from the City of Shadow is legendary among the Kharadron Overlords. Tales abound of their use of specially modified optical arrays that can alter the colour of their ships, and of surprise attacks launched suddenly by their fleets from clouds of unnatural blackness.

To the unease of its rivals, Barak-Mhornar recently became the first sky-port with delegates on the Geldraad to abandon Chamon. Contact was lost with the City of Shadow, and exploratory fleets sent to investigate found it entirely missing, a swirling portal of umbral magic in its place. The only way to access Barak-Mhornar is to pass through this mysterious Realmgate, which leads to a labyrinthine archipelago of mist-shrouded isles with the sky-port at its centre. Traders are still granted access to carry out illicit transactions, escorted through the maze by black-hulled ships. Despite the Geldraad's urgings, the Admirals of Barak-Mhornar steadfastedly refuse to reveal the city's true location.

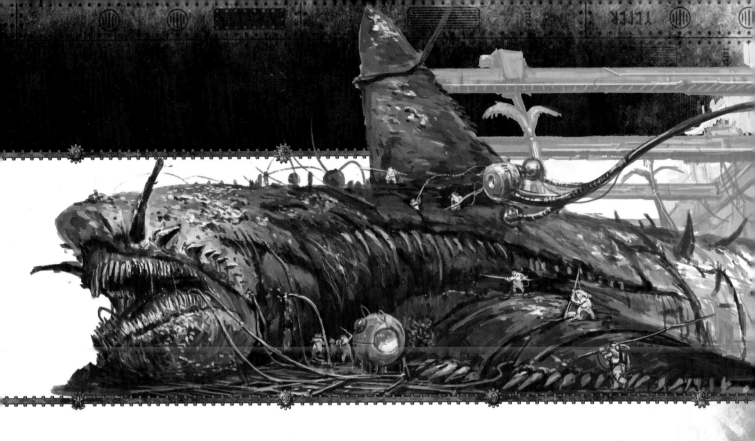

BARAK-ZILFIN

Barak-Zilfin, the Windswept City, is famed for the skill of its pilots and shipwrights. No fleets venture as far as those from this sky-port, and while some regard them as reckless, they are supremely confident in the abilities of their crew and the sturdiness of their ships.

None can predict or ride the aetheric currents as the airfleets of Barak-Zilfin can. Within wider Kharadron society they are known as the 'Windmasters', although the other sky-ports claim this moniker refers to the fact that they are all blowhards – or even that duardin from the sky-port tend to suffer from advanced flatulence. The citizens of Barak-Zilfin simply laugh off such petty insults as simple jealousy, for the aggressive opening of

new trade markets has seen the Windswept City grow to be the second largest of the Kharadron sky-ports, holding vital seats on the Geldraad. It is a position they seem unlikely to relinquish, for the Great Coghalls of Barak-Zilfin – the most famed of all Endrineering Academies – produce more new airships than any other.

Of all the sky-ports, Barak-Zilfin gained the most from the confusion and Chaos caused by the Garaktormun. Not only did they manage to increase their shares sufficiently to earn an additional seat on the Geldraad, but the sky-port's expert Aetheric Navigators were able to guide the city's fleets safely through the worst of the cyclonic storms.

BARAK-THRYNG

The old ways are best, say the duardin of Barak-Thryng. They are so conservative that they feel the Kharadron Code should not be altered from its original form, and they even stubbornly refuse to recognise some of the amendments that have been made since. Such an outlook has meant that they have a garnered a reputation within Kharadron society as intractable trading partners. Obstreperous and easily offended, the folk of Barak-Thryng venerate the past and fill their city with monuments to the duardin's ancestors and gods. Their disposition is best described as gruff, and even amongst fellow duardin they are infamous for holding grudges. Although they have but a single delegate in the Geldraad – the hoary Admiral Grymm Sternbok – none can fail to hear his loud list of complaints at every session.

The City of the Ancestors' obstinate adherence to the old traditions actually proved to be a boon during the Great Gale of Death. The aether-gold mines of Barak-Thryng are distinct – other, wealthier sky-ports would probably say 'quaint' – in that they rely upon archaic endrin-bellows to steadily suck in great gouts of the substance; a process that is far slower than more recent mining methods developed by the Kharadron, but is much less wasteful. As a result of this trademark thriftiness, the masters of Barak-Thryng had a sizeable reserve of the Breath of Grungni stockpiled for emergencies, and were able to ride out the worst of the necroquake's effects. The city's venerable grumblers have since taken great delight in reminding their flashier kin of this at every possible opportunity.

BARAK-ZON

The first founded of the sky-ports, Barak-Zon is also the highest situated. It is known as the City of the Sun because the light of Hysh causes the floating metal metropolis to gleam red from afar, as though it were burning like some distant star. Fourteen triumphal arches are situated throughout the sky-port, each marking a major victory of its people. Martial pride is everything to its citizens, and rare indeed is the Barak-Zon Arkanaut who does not long to earn the Ironstar and be immortalised on one of the many avenues of heroes that traverse the city. The duardin of Barak-Zon hail the indomitable Admiral Nelriksson as their greatest champion, for it was he who famously triumphed at the Battle of Tungsten Peaks during the Time of Reaving.

In recent years, expeditionary forces from Barak-Zon have found profitable work as hired soldiers, combatting the steady rise in ethereal and daemonic threats in exchange for lucrative trading and mining rights. The other sky-ports typically look down on this propensity for mercenary work, but Barak-Zon's Grundcorps and Arkanaut Companies have no such qualms. One notable campaign launched by the city saw the 37th Expeditionary Sky-fleet under Admiral Caber Rasmus fight at the Siege of Fort Talburnia, defending the Freeguild stronghold against the Spiderfang Stalktribes of Zigtik Seven-legs. Only eighteen Grundstok Thunderers out of two hundred survived, each earning the Ironstar for their brave service.

BARAK-NAR

The City of the First Sunrise, Barak-Nar is the largest and most successful of the Kharadron sky-ports. It is they who have the Steering Hand, for they have the most delegates upon the ruling council of the Geldraad. The denizens of Barak-Nar are highly practical and the least superstitious of their kind. The city is best known for its many leading science academies, its great wealth and its history of producing dynamic leaders. Bold, fearless and progressive, the folk of Barak-Nar were the first of the Kharadron Overlords to aggressively pursue trade agreements with non-duardin settlements, and it was they who established the best-patrolled trade routes, routinely marking the sky-paths with zonbeks: well-garrisoned lighthouse docks.

The necroquake hit Barak-Nar hard, for many of its most profitable aether-streams were swept away upon roaring gales of magic. Such was the economic strain on the sky-port in the wake of the event that they even lost a seat on the Geldraad, something that would have been unthinkable before the disaster. Yet despite this setback, canny manoeuvring by the remaining delegates of Barak-Nar meant that a number of trading monopolies were soon secured over newly discovered seams. Aether-gold is once more beginning to pour into the sky-port's vaults at a swiftly gathering pace, and the city's Admirals Council has decreed scores of new voyages into unexplored regions of Chamon, charting new sky-paths and laying claim to prosperous new territories.

ADMIRALS AND WARRANT OFFICERS

A skyvessel is only as strong as its warrant officers, so the saying goes, and veterans of the Arkanaut companies will attest to its accuracy. Having earned their commission through hard work and ruthless profiteering, these seasoned commanders are responsible for leading their crews to fortune and glory.

LORD-MAGNATE BROKK GRUNGSSON

Brokk Grungsson exemplifies the self-made Kharadron Overlord privateer. He is rapacious in the hunt for aether-gold, and daring in his explorations of the skybound wonders of Chamon. Brokk Grungsson is the only Admiral that has successfully led a fleet around the fabled Horn of Chamon. He is hailed as the victor of the Battle of Stratis Skull, and when all the sky-ports joined forces to break the siege of Barak-Zon it was Brokk who was elected as the combined fleets' High Admiral.

The son of a humble dock worker, Grungsson's rise to the heights of power is nothing short of remarkable. Beginning his career as an Arkanaut, his boldness, strategic mastery and ruthless business savvy saw him rapidly climb the ranks. After only a decade's service, he had secured his own captaincy, and after winning a stunning victory over greenskin corsairs on the island of Madralta, he was granted the position of Lord-Magnate – the highest rank a Kharadron can achieve without holding a place on the Admirals Council, and one that has allowed him to gather a fortune in aether-gold shares.

Putting his growing wealth to use, Brokk commissioned a magnificent custom-built dirigible suit from the Master Endrineer Durek Coghammer of Barak-Zilfin. This aether-powered exo-armour not only grants Brokk the power of flight but also incorporates a number of advanced weapons, including a pair of moustache-mounted aetherblasters, a multi-barrelled gun he refers to as the Magnate's Charter and a sizable cannon called Grungsson's Boast. Brokk's preferred strategy is to issue the fleet commands before leading his Skyriggers on bold manoeuvres to vanquish the greatest threat amongst the enemy's number, be it commander, ship or monster.

ARKANAUT ADMIRALS

An Arkanaut Admiral is the leader of an airfleet. An Admiral does not have a ship of his own, as each ship has a Captain at the wheel, but will nominate one craft as his flagship. It takes success and tremendous profit for a duardin to catapult themselves into the upper echelons of the airfleets, and individuals that have done so are battle-scarred veterans that have seen countless wars, boarding actions and aerial bombardments.

The majority of Admirals have worked their way up through the ranks after first joining the sky-fleets as neophyte Arkanauts. This gives them an appreciation for the less glamorous tasks that are required to keep a vessel afloat as well as a knowledge of essential aeronautical skills. In order to progress from Captain to Admiral, they must pass an exhaustive examination involving both theoretical and practical tests, including a final hearing in front of the assembled Admirals Council of their home port. Only upon a majority vote from their superiors will they be confirmed, by which point their knowledge of shipcraft, military theory and – perhaps most importantly – the Kharadron Code is encyclopaedic.

Whether ordering tactical manoeuvres, directing concentrated firepower or coordinating land and air forces, an Arkanaut Admiral is first and foremost a leader. Yet Admirals do not earn their rank by issuing commands alone, nor do they lead from the rear. Using their high share of profits, an Admiral can outfit themselves with thick plates of Arkanaut armour and back-mounted generators that fuel their aethermatically powered skalfhammer, enabling it to impact with enough force to crack boulders. A sidearm is standard, typically a multi-barrelled volley pistol.

ENDRINMASTERS

Only a Kharadron who has proved their mech-mastery and ability to safeguard a fleet's investments can hope to rise to the rank of Endrinmaster. As senior members of the Endrineers Guild, these veteran technicians are responsible for the upkeep of an expedition skyvessel. It is a duty in which they take great pride, and each Endrinmaster is keen to demonstrate the exemplary quality of the craft in their charge.

Endrinmasters are adept at performing complex field repairs even under the most harrowing of circumstances, but they are also capable warriors. An Endrinmaster's maintenance tools often serve just as well as weapons of war. Many carry aethermight hammers, weapons of such weight that only by fitting a strength-enhancing endrinharness to a duardin's armour can they be wielded at all. Others employ manipulators and drills used for delicate repairs to tear apart enemies, all the while raining death from afar with a trusty aethercannon. Common to all Endrinmasters is the God's Eye, a lens-array that is capable of emitting a powerful and deadly energy beam.

While a sky-fleet often has one Endrinmaster assigned to its flagship, others are tasked with overseeing maintenance and repairs for the rest of the flotilla. These Endrinmasters often don dirigible harnesses powered by whirring aether-turbines, sturdy one-duardin endrins that allow them to soar alongside their cherished skyvessel and respond quickly to any mechanical issues.

AETHERIC NAVIGATORS

Masters of the guiding winds, Aetheric Navigators are aero-cartographers, atmospheric map-makers that help chart courses, find currents and steer along perilous trade routes. They are the eyes and ears of the sky-fleet, and even the most journeyed Admirals value their sage counsel. Woe betide any privateer captain foolish enough to embark upon a long and dangerous journey into hostile territory without an experienced Aetheric Navigator at their side.

Equipped with a bewildering variety of multispectral ocular lenses, each attuned to the ever-shifting winds of magic, Navigators can visualise a variety of aetheric phenomena. They can identify barometric eddies and electro-aetheric vortices and can plot a course through such hazards with ease. Using a plethora of mechanical wonders, an Aetheric Navigator can also influence the winds to gain the weather gauge, speed up his fleet or slow down flying foes by buffeting them with heavy gales.

Aetheric Navigators can even call upon the aetheric currents to disrupt enemy spells. Though Navigators possess no arcane power of their own, their strange science provides an effective counter to enemy wizards. The winds of the realms are inextricably linked to the flow of magic and, when manipulated carefully, can smother an arcane flame or bolt of lightning before it can fully manifest. Should a foe of any description attempt to interfere in this complex process, a heavy ranging pistol provides adequate discouragement.

AETHER-KHEMISTS

An Aether-Khemist is an invaluable addition to an airfleet. The armour worn by these specialists incorporates an array of high-tech tools, including quadbreather apparatus that allows them to – almost literally – sniff out aether-gold hidden within thick cloudbanks. An Aether-Khemist's nose for the stuff is so uncannily accurate that those Admirals who hire one of these alchemical experts at great expense almost always see their investment returned manyfold.

Although their primary roles are those of prospectors and arcane scientists, Aether-Khemists are trained for battle and armed with several deadly tools. In addition to harvesting and assessing airborne resources, their atmospheric anatomisers can vacuum away a foe's breathable air or spray a billowing cloud of lethal chemicals. Pressurised gouts of poison gas can be fired forwards in a deafening blast known as the 'Roar of Grungni'. Should the enemy press too close, the Aether-Khemist's sturdy equipment serves as a crude but effective bludgeon.

Although quite capable in combat, Aether-Khemists generally prefer to rely on accompanying Arkanauts to clear away hostiles from rich harvesting zones. Indeed, their atomisers have an additional feature designed to maximise the killing power of their comrades' guns. With the pull of a lever, a shimmering golden cloud of chem-fog is released – a metallic fug that boosts the armour-piercing effectiveness of nearby aetheric weapons.

IRONCLADS AND SKYRIGGERS

Arkanaut Ironclads are the heavily armed lynchpins around which the Kharadron airfleets are formed. Each is a juggernaut of a vessel, bristling with cannon, bombs and heavily armed duardin marines. The Skyriggers are specialised units with flight-capable aether-endrins whose task it is to ensure the fleet remains in fighting shape.

ARKANAUT IRONCLADS

An Ironclad is a devastating engine of war, a bulky and formidably resilient ship of the line possessing sufficient firepower to level a city. When one of these monsters hoves into view, bringing to bear a bristling array of guns and torpedo launchers, the enemy has a few short moments to ponder the certainty of their doom before the Ironclad unleashes a thunderous barrage of explosive death upon them. Ironclads form the core of most Kharadron airfleets and are the largest vessels routinely fielded by the sky-ports. They are certainly not the biggest aether-powered monsters to take to the skies – there exist immense battleships and wing-carriers many times an Ironclad's size – but these centrepiece machines are far too costly to produce en masse. In the Ironclad, the sky-ports have found a superb balance of offensive capability and aether-gold consumption that has yet to be improved upon.

A single Ironclad represents a significant outlay for even the wealthiest sky-port, and thus they are built with endurance and efficiency foremost in mind. With enough hold space to store a vast bounty of aether-gold, as well as scores of Arkanauts and Grundstok Thunderers, Ironclads are designed to operate in the field for many seasons, relying upon their iron-riveted, reinforced hulls and the tender care of their Endrinmasters to keep them in perfect fighting shape. Yet for all the Ironclad's defensive capability, the master Endrineers of the sky-ports understand that the best defence is an utterly overwhelming offence. Batteries of bow-mounted swivelguns pound nearby enemies with solid shot. Aethershock torpedoes powered by miniature jet-endrins leave smoking contrails as they race towards their target before detonating in a blossoming fireball, while ground targets are obliterated by rack upon rack of grudgesettler bombs. The most destructive tool at an Ironclad Captain's disposal is typically mounted on the forecastle – either a great sky cannon or great skyhook for blasting larger enemies out of the sky, or a great volley cannon for raking enemy hordes with a deadly hail of aethershot.

ENDRINRIGGERS

Endrinriggers are one of two types of airborne troop designated by the Kharadron as 'Skyriggers'. Defined by their bulbous back-mounted aether-endrins, these duardin are capable of taking flight alongside the sky-fleets or hitching themselves to vessels with mag-boots or skyhooks in order to conserve fuel. When battle is joined, Skyrigger teams will detach from the ship's hull and serve as rapid-response units.

Endrinriggers are primarily charged with the maintenance of a sky-fleet's vessels. As junior members of the Endrineers Guild, they report directly to the fleet's Admiral and Endrinmaster. In the Kharadron's meritocratic society, advancement to a guild's upper echelons can only be achieved through feats of competence and daring in the line of duty. Driven by a need to prove their worth, Endrinriggers will dart through intense danger to reach stricken vessels, performing complex field repairs while the carnage roars on around them. The repair tools carried by Endrinriggers can prove lethal when turned upon the foe. Red-hot rivets fired by handheld pistols can pierce flesh and armour just as easily as they punch through the hull of an airship. When the enemy presses in close, aethermatic saws are used to methodically and messily dismember them. Some Endrinriggers even make use of grapnel launchers to haul enemies out of cover, dragging them into the open to be mown down in a hail of aethershot.

SKYWARDENS

Formed of elite Arkanaut crews, Skywardens are the second of the two Skyrigger configurations common across all Kharadron fleets. Soaring through the air with the aid of their single-pilot aether-endrins, Skywardens function as airborne shock troops rather than dedicated combat mechanics. They descend to disrupt enemy formations and strike at vulnerable targets before employing their superior mobility to avoid retribution. As a further deterrent, Skywarden units are equipped with skymines and timed charges. Enemies who attempt to give pursuit must navigate a murderous field of drifting explosives, and one misstep could see them blown to smithereens.

The weapons carried by Skywarden teams suit their role as aerial cavalry. Vulcaniser pistols are short-ranged but deadly sidearms that fire superheated blasts of aether. Even the heaviest armour can be reduced to molten slag by concentrated vulcaniser fire. Enemies reeling under this barrage are easy prey for other Skywardens carrying skypikes. Each skypike is taller than the duardin who bears it; when propelled by both its whirring aether-powered engines and the strength of its wielder's arm, a well-aimed skypike can tear through an ogor's belly-plate with a single blow.

FRIGATES AND COMPANIES

The Arkanaut Frigate has become a potent symbol of Kharadron military might. Sleek and swift, they carve through the skies like megalofins on the hunt, blasting their enemy with lethal broadsides before descending to deliver their Arkanaut Companies into the thick of battle.

ARKANAUT FRIGATES

The Arkanaut Frigate represents centuries of refinement by the shipwrights of the Endrineers Guild. In its design, a balance was struck between speed, transport capacity and firepower to create a versatile craft that could serve as the mainstay for the airfleets. With its sleek hull and powerful buoyancy endrin, the Arkanaut Frigate is fast enough to escape a ravenous lumprey and has enough power to pull clear from the gravitational drag of a density hole.

While a Frigate's cargo holds are tiny compared to the massive aetherhulks or cloud-dredgers used for mining, these craft carry few weapons and move at a speed that can barely cause a flag to ripple. Among the core vessels of the airfleets, only the Arkanaut Ironclad bears more firepower than the Frigate. The Frigate's main gun is mounted atop the foredeck in a turret that can be fitted with either a sky cannon or a harpoon-like skyhook, weapons as devastating in war as they are in the Kharadron's hunts for the monstrous creatures that prowl the sky-ways above Chamon.

Bow-mounted ball turrets house aethershot swivelguns, their high-velocity salvoes laying down a deadly spray of shot, and the craft's payload of grudgesettler bombs can lay waste to tightly packed ground targets. Should attackers attempt to board the Frigate, detonation drills are released, tearing up the terrain in a chain of seismic blasts to stop the enemy's manoeuvres in their tracks. The ship is similarly well defended against aerial threats – many a harkraken tentacle has snaked out of the clouds seeking to grasp an Arkanaut Frigate, only to be repelled by exploding skymines.

Arkanaut Frigates can be found throughout the airfleets. They form the backbone of the patrols that secure the airspace around every major sky-port. For lesser trade ventures, Arkanaut Frigates may even haul goods, although typically they act as escorts to the trade fleets. In small-scale mining operations, Arkanaut Frigates perform all the associated ship duties – hunting aether-gold seams, cloud dredging and siphoning, and transporting the unrefined gases. In larger operations, the Arkanaut Frigates are still used but their role centres around protecting the vulnerable mining trawlers and tankers. Yet the versatile nature of the Arkanaut Frigate should not distract from the fact that the Kharadron Overlords designed it as a ship of war, and it is in battle where the craft truly excels.

During the breaking of the blockade of Barak-Zon, Arkanaut Frigates of all the sky-ports assumed a line abreast formation. They poured forth such firepower that not only was the arcane chain that threatened to strangle the floating city broken, but the flying daemon hosts were utterly obliterated. Beasts and tribesmen alike throughout the Kharzdon Mountains looked skyward to see strange flickering lights, ignorant of the fact that the phenomenon was caused by the daemons' spectacular doom, visible even in broad daylight. Even a trio of Arkanaut Frigates possesses a terrifying amount of firepower, as was proven at the battle over Grimlock Pass. There, a small fleet out of Barak-Nar was enough to break the charge of Waaagh! Ironteef, saving several mountaintop trading posts in that region. No greenskins have dared enter the pass since.

ARKANAUT COMPANIES

Despite the overwhelming firepower of the airfleets, all Admirals know that to secure territory, infantry is needed. When it comes to feet on the ground, the Arkanaut Companies form the Kharadron Overlords' main fighting forces. Descending swiftly via a Frigate's grav-ladders or suspension ropes, an Arkanaut Company can deploy rapidly into the fray. Most are armed with pistols and stout cutting blades, allowing them to pepper the enemy with shots before engaging them at close quarters. A few of the Arkanauts carry heavier weaponry – a skypike adds to a company's close-combat prowess, an aethermatic volley gun lays down a blisteringly high rate of fire, while the portable version of the ship-mounted skyhook is effective at bringing down large targets.

The Arkanaut Companies are a hardened lot, toughened not only by battle but also the daily challenge of aeronautical life. They spend whole wind cycles at a time aboard their craft, crammed into tight quarters. What seemed like easy sailing can become a treacherous journey with little warning, whether owing to sudden and severe climatic change or attacks from airborne raiders and monsters. Simply standing watch at high altitude is an ordeal, for even within Arkanaut armour a duardin becomes wind-bitten, their skin hardened by the strange metallic airs that drift far above the clouds of Chamon. Special rebreathers built into their helms and masks filter toxic vapours as the Arkanauts work long shifts scanning the horizon for foes, searching for the telltale shimmer of aether-gold veins or watching out for the oncoming specks that can all too quickly resolve into roaring packs of manticores. Every black cloud that passes might harbour a harkraken, and enemy fleets – from those of rogue sky-ports to airborne grots – can attack from any angle.

VESSELS OF RENOWN

In the annals of the Kharadron Overlords, there are countless examples of how the actions of a single skyvessel have changed the course of history. The names of these ships echo through the ages, and tales of their exploits and the heroism of their Captains inspire the next generation of Kharadron aeronauts.

Perhaps the most famous vessel of all is the Arkanaut Frigate *Nazgrund* ('Cloudhammer'), the legendary flagship of Horgrumm Brand, first of the Kharadron Grand Admirals. The most cutting-edge example of Kharadron aeronautical endrineering of its time, the *Nazgrund* fought at the Battle of the First Coalition, in which a newly united Kharadron armada smashed the skyborne hosts of the Tetronomicar, three Daemon Princes who had pursued the sky-ports ever since they first took off from their former mountain homes. Though he masterminded a stunning victory against overwhelming odds, Grand Admiral Brand fell during that engagement, his flesh turned to silver by a bolt

of witchfire from a Lord of Change's staff. To honour his sacrifice, Brand's metal body was mounted to the *Nazgrund*'s prow as a figurehead. The vessel was subsequently piloted by many famous Captains and Admirals, and after centuries of service, it now takes pride of place in the Ancestor's Plaza of Barak-Nar. Rumour has it that the sky-port's Endrineers Guild has equipped the venerable Frigate with the latest aether-jet endrins and an arsenal of experimental weaponry, and it stands ready to once more lead the City of the First Sunrise into battle in their darkest hour.

Each sky-port has its own heroes. *Rhyngul Vengryn* ('Redmetal Vengeance'), the flagship of Captain Grund Tahlihro, so-called Master of the Outer Airs, is known by every beardling in Barak-Zon. Songs are still sung in Barak-Mhornar extolling the deeds of the infamous Zayn Reggsson and his Ironclad *Night's Gift*, while Admiral Ebbrig Ahl-Kalim of Barak-Zilfin mapped more of the great sky-lanes than any other port aboard his Arkanaut Frigate *Trailblazer*.

Despite the many dangers of life on the sky-ways, there are always more duardin who wish to become Arkanauts, eager for their chance to earn great wealth. In the days of the Sky Exodus, the growing airfleets were crewed by clans. When the Code was established, however, meritocracy supplanted the old ways, and so recruiting practices changed. Those who served in the Arkanaut Companies were not simply able bodies connected by blood, they were the boldest of their kind.

On the day of Brynruf – when the sun shines gold over Chamon – the different Arkanaut Academies of every sky-port hold a six-day competition. Only the highest achievers are allowed into the Arkanaut Academies, the training facilities where airfleet veterans conduct military drills and teach aeronautical skills. On Musterpress days, Captains arrive to observe the drills, and they may choose to recruit new crew members by purchasing contracts, often to fill the places that have become available through death or injury. Those selected to join the Arkanaut Companies will endure any number of rites and rituals sacred to their new fleet, ship or both. Those passed over after three Musterpresses must instead settle for lesser positions, often on mining or fishing vessels or as dockworkers.

THE GRUNDCORPS

To ensure the protection of their ship and the safeguarding of their cargo, Kharadron officers turn to the professional soldiers of the Grundcorps. Oathsigned into contracts of service and wielding a blistering array of weapons, these grizzled duardin put their lives on the line in the name of profit and glory.

To the Kharadron Overlords, the name Grundstok is synonymous with elite military prowess. In exchange for a charter and shares in the fleets' profits, the Grundstok Company – sometimes called the Grundcorps – sends their highly trained warriors and escort fighter craft to safeguard the airfleets. Founded soon after the Sky Exodus, the rise of the Grundcorps has paralleled the growth of the burgeoning empire of the Kharadron Overlords.

Now, their training academies can be found in all major sky-ports, and even some minor ones. Their mission has remained the same since they were established by Belegrimm Grundstok, in the days when he trained units of crack shots. Their motto, 'kazar valrhank', means 'protect with honour'. It is a duty they evidently perform well, for Grundcorps business is flourishing.

GRUNDSTOK THUNDERERS

The Grundstok Thunderers are militarised formations employed by the fleet to provide defence against hostile forces. While their main task is to repel boarders with vicious, close-range firepower, they are equally comfortable operating in the field. The endless training and drilling conducted by the Grundstok Academies results in high standards of discipline and marksmanship in their graduates – upon commands from their officer, the Grundcaptain, they march, wheel and ready their aim with awe-inspiring speed and precision. Firing in near-perfect synchronicity, a line of Grundstok Thunderers temporarily disappears among eye-searing flashes and weapon reports as they unleash a storm of munitions that can halt even the most well-armoured foes in their tracks.

The Grundstok Company spares no expense in outfitting their warriors, and each is equipped with the finest arms and armour available to the Kharadron Overlords. Aethershot rifles shoot a hypercharged blast of aether that condenses mid-flight into a solid round, combining a high rate of fire with impressive stopping power. The aethercannon operates on a similar principle but is a heftier model that fires rounds of a much larger calibre. The aetheric fumigator belches forth a cloud of noxious fumes, while the multi-barrelled decksweeper fires a wide spray of aether-grain shot, ideal for repelling enemy boarding actions. Meanwhile, the Grundstok mortar lobs a high-arcing shell that terminates in a blinding explosion of lethal aether-energies. With such a versatile combination of arms at their disposal, there is no combat situation that the Thunderers are not equipped to deal with.

Grundstok Thunderer formations often include an Honour Bearer, a warrior carrying an ancestral standard that holds a record of the unit's proud history. Furthermore, it is tradition for units to be accompanied by an aethermatic bird known as a drillbill, in honour of the original that was taken to battle by Grundstok himself. Grundstok Thunderers are transported aboard an Arkanaut Frigate or Ironclad, forming an invaluable reserve that can be deployed quickly to wherever they are needed. Kharadron military history is replete with stories of Thunderers arriving in the nick of time to solidify a battle line or drive back an encroaching enemy, standing alone at battle's end surrounded by a circle of fallen foes.

Notoriously proud of their martial heritage, Grundstok marines are not shy about extolling their own skill in battle, nor do they hold back when criticising the marksmanship and general soldiery of their Arkanaut comrades. This occasionally causes friction between the two groups, but all is forgiven when battle calls, for even the most truculent Arkanaut has a grudging respect for the manner in which the Grundcorps methodically obliterates its foes.

GRUNDSTOK GUNHAULERS

Roving the skies in tight formations, Grundstok Gunhaulers are one of the fastest classes of vessel found among the Kharadron sky-fleets. Each Gunhauler is a two-duardin attack craft, propelled by a single buoyancy endrin and armed with an array of deadly main and secondary armaments.

Unlike the Frigates and Ironclads that comprise the Kharadron ships of the line, Gunhaulers belong not to the Arkanaut fleets but to the Grundstok Company. Primarily employed to protect the errant sky-fleets, the military contractors of the Grundstok Company offer the services of Gunhaulers as escort vessels. These craft – nimble in comparison to their charges – provide fire support alongside the heavier vessels of a fleet and take advantage of their speed to proactively seek out and obliterate threats.

Gunhaulers switch between these two roles according to the commands of their Admiral. When on the offensive, they are typically tasked with eliminating single targets. Doggedly seeking out their prey, Gunhaulers dart through the chaos of battle before blasting the unlucky foe to shreds with booming sky cannons and armour-penetrating drill cannon rounds. Though they have the profile of escort ships rather than sleek fighter craft, these swift vessels are capable of surprising feats of agility in the hands of a skilled pilot – and the Grundstok Academies have no shortage of those.

When escorting larger skyvessels, the Grundstok Gunhaulers prove just as adept. Each crewman has been relentlessly drilled in the importance of safeguarding their sister ships – after all, both the reputation and the profits of the Grundstok Company depend upon it. Gunhauler pilots will employ their craft's impressive agility to interdict airborne enemies or, in dire circumstances, position themselves to physically absorb an incoming attack. Escort vessels they may be, but Gunhaulers are still sturdy, duardin-made constructs, able to endure heavy damage and fight on. In times of need, a Gunhauler can divert more power to its aether-endrins, flying high to reposition itself before descending from above once more with guns blazing in a blistering attack run.

Arkanaut Narvi Gundersson watched, grim-faced, as hundreds of skittering shapes surged towards the beacon tower.

'Present,' roared Captain Drumm, and a dozen exhausted and bloody privateers of Barak-Zon rose above the parapet, guns aimed.

'This time it'll come down to steel,' Drumm said, as the wretched things drew ever closer. 'Make it count, boys. There'll be a plot in Heroes' Rise for each and all of us!'

Narvi cheered along with the rest, but he could not help but think of what might have been. It was a mighty haul of aether-gold they'd sniffed out. A 'career-maker', the Captain had called it.

Looking out at the carpet of chitinous bodies, Narvi guessed that his own, nascent career was about to come to an abrupt and violent end.

'Grobkaz,' he cursed, and as Captain Drumm bellowed the order to fire, he sighted the nearest spider and gave it a mouthful of aethershot.

The thing's head came apart in a spray of ichor and gristle, its rider tumbling away squealing. A ripple of gunfire scythed down dozens more of the spiders, then the scuttling abominations spilled over the ramparts and the slaughter began.

Narvi heard the screams of dying shipmates. A stray, green-fletched arrow caught him in the thigh and he sank to his knees with a groan. Rearing over the parapet came a long-limbed arachnoid nightmare, its many eyes peering at him greedily.

Career over, Narvi had time to think.

Then the creature burst apart, splattering him with gooey, yellow slime.

'What in Grungni's name?' he muttered, rolling onto his elbows and staring up at the crimson sky to see a squadron of Grundstok Gunhaulers roar overhead, strafing away at the mass of spiders with their hull-mounted swivelguns.

Scrabbling to his feet, Narvi grinned as an Arkanaut Frigate soared in behind the Gunhaulers, disgorging squads of heavily armed Thunderers from its metal hatches. Levelling large-bore cannons and aethershot rifles, the Grundstok marines fired a deadly accurate volley that cleared the edge of the rampart and another that turned a score more arachnids into glistening mulch.

'Wonderful,' said Captain Drumm, spitting a mouthful of chewed-up blackleaf over the edge of the battlement. 'Saved by the glory-seekers. We'll never hear the end of this.'

Surging forth from the clouds come the Kharadron Overlords, strafing their daemonic foes with raking streams of aethershot and spiralling torpedoes.

DEATH FROM ABOVE

There are few more astonishing and imposing sights in the Mortal Realms than that of a Kharadron sky-fleet bursting forth from the clouds, sunlight glinting upon the polished endrinspheres of huge iron warships and the guns of airborne privateers as they descend upon their foes.

The Kharadron Overlords attack in tight formation, heavy Ironclads and Frigates providing a core of overwhelming firepower while endrin-equipped Skyriggers and swift Grundstok Gunhaulers clear out enemy infantry.

Brokk Grungsson,
Lord-Magnate of Barak-Nar

Aetheric Navigator   Aether-Khemist   Arkanaut Admiral   Endrinmaster

Enrik Ironhail   Garodd Alensen   Bjorgen Thundrik   Dead-Eye Lund   Khazgan Drakkskewer

Thundrik's Profiteers are a band of hard-bitten, gunslinging Kharadron privateers who have travelled far across the deadly wilds of the realms in search of a career-making score.

Endrinmaster with Dirigible Suit

An Endrinmaster and his loyal crew of Skyriggers launch an assault upon territory held by the Disciples of Tzeentch, sweeping down upon their sorcerous foes with guns blazing.

It is an Endrinrigger's duty not only to conduct combat repairs on the fleet's skyvessels, but also to respond to emerging threats – such as rampaging, boulder-hurling Cygors – with volleys of aethershot and glowing-hot rivets.

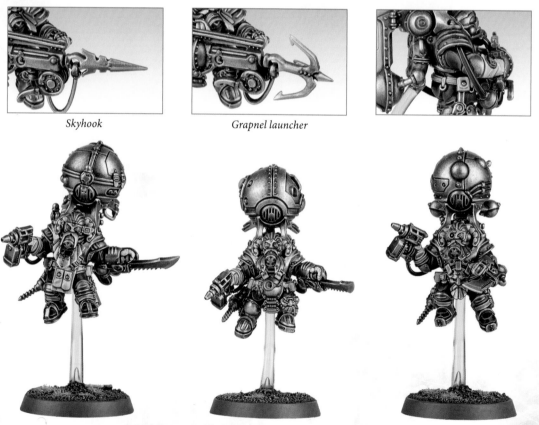

Skyhook

Grapnel launcher

Endrinriggers with rapid-fire rivet guns and aethermatic saws

Company Captain with
volley pistol

Company Captain with
aetherflare pistol

Arkanaut Company

Arkanaut with skypike

Arkanaut with
aethermatic volley gun

Arkanaut with light skyhook

Arkanaut Company

An Aether-Khemist leads a platoon of heavily armed Kharadron infantry into the sweltering jungles of Invidia, following
a trail of aether-gold into lands infested with skittering, arachnid horrors.

Skyvessel bomb racks carry a variety of warheads.

Crew-operated aethershot carbine

Grundstok Gunhauler

Grundstok Thunderer with decksweeper

Grundstok Thunderer with Grundstok mortar

Grundstok Thunderer with aethercannon

Honour Bearer

Grundstok Thunderer with aethershot rifle

Gunnery Sergeant

Grundstok Thunderer with aetheric fumigator

An Arkanaut Admiral, seeing his expeditionary fleet outnumbered by throngs of bloodthirsty Slaves to Darkness, calls upon the devastating firepower of the Grundstok Thunderers to even the odds.

The Spiral Crux is a land ravaged by arcane storms of terrible power and dominated by the Disciples of Tzeentch, but its vast reserves of aether-gold are far too tempting a prize for the Kharadron sky-ports to ignore.

Ancestor figurehead

Arkanaut Frigate

Arkanaut Ironclad

The veteran Captain of a bulky Arkanaut Ironclad skilfully guides his vessel through a narrow canyon before unleashing a devastating salvo of fire into a swirl of Nighthaunt gheists.

PRIDE OF THE SKY-PORTS

The Kharadron Overlords organise their vessels into airfleets, each built around a core of mighty ships of the line but also containing a variety of swift escort gunships and firearm-wielding infantry. There are many ways to collect a Kharadron army, but below you will find an example of a coherent, themed collection.

There's no right way or wrong way to go about collecting a Kharadron Overlords army. You might like the look of a particular model, such as the imposing Arkanaut Ironclad, with its complement of gleaming cannons. Alternatively, you might take a look through the warscrolls in the battletome and opt to choose units that seem particularly well suited to your playstyle. However you choose to go about it, the end goal is always the same: to create a mighty host of battle-hardened privateers ready to take to the skies in search of profit and glory!

An Arkanaut Admiral was the obvious choice of leader for our Barak-Zilfin airfleet. As befits his lofty rank, the Admiral wears one of the most advanced battle-rigs available to a duardin of the skies, and wields a formidable pair of weapons in the form of an armour-busting skalfhammer and rapid-firing volley pistol, making him more than capable of holding his own in both ranged shoot-outs and close combat. He also has access to several powerful command abilities, making him an invaluable force multiplier.

As with any airfleet worth its salt, our army boasts a number of specialists and warrant officers to cover all our tactical needs. An Aetheric Navigator will enable our airships and flying units to cover even more ground, while an Aether-Khemist can further boost the killing power of aethershot weapons. Since we have a hefty number of vessels to take care of, we have added not one but two Endrinmasters – one with a dirigible suit that will allow him to soar across the skies and quickly reach any stricken vessels.

Speaking of skyvessels, we have liberally sprinkled these into our army. A mighty Arkanaut Ironclad is an incredible showpiece model, and can transport our infantry units directly into the heart of battle. Two Arkanaut Frigates provide intense firepower and further transport capacity, while three Grundstok Gunhaulers can run interference and respond to any emerging threats.

Every army benefits from a strong core of infantry, and we have chosen two Arkanaut Companies to lead the line. These will start each battle in the hold of the Frigates, ready to jump out and enter the fray as necessary. A unit of elite Grundstok Thunderers adds much-appreciated firepower, with a variety of weapons capable of wiping out even the toughest targets. The elite aerial cavalry known as Skywardens are ready to respond swiftly with their skypikes and volley guns. These warriors can latch onto the larger vessels in order to greatly increase their speed, and also pack an explosive surprise for pursuers in the form of skymines and timed charges.

Though they also wear aether-endrins, Endrinriggers offer a more defensive option. These trained mechanics conduct on-the-spot airborne repairs, though if necessary they can turn their high-powered tools upon their enemies.

Offering a potent blend of speed and firepower, our Barak-Zilfin airfleet will be able to outmanoeuvre and pick their foes apart, earning a bounteous score of precious aether-gold in the process!

1. Arkanaut Admiral
2. Aether-Khemist
3. Aetheric Navigator
4. Endrinmaster with Dirigible Suit
5. Endrinmaster with Endrinharness
6. Arkanaut Ironclad
7. Arkanaut Frigate
8. Grundstok Gunhaulers
9. Arkanaut Company
10. Grundstok Thunderers
11. Skywardens
12. Endrinriggers

'There comes a time in every Arkanaut's career when you have to straighten your beard and roll the dhrazba. No one ever made their fortune by playing things safe.'
- Lord-Magnate Brokk Grungsson of Barak-Nar

PAINTING YOUR KHARADRON OVERLORDS

The airfleets of the Kharadron Overlords make for a spectacular sight upon the battlefield, a gleaming fusion of technology and arcane science. Whether you are a brand-new painter approaching your first ever collection, or a veteran brush-wielder, the following tips and tricks will help you to get the best from your models.

One of the most enjoyable aspects of the Games Workshop hobby is taking paint and brush and bringing your collection of Citadel Miniatures to life. Even a single model looks fantastic when carefully painted and based. However, nothing beats gathering your miniatures together into a fully painted tabletop army upon the field of battle and seeing the impressive spectacle they present.

Painting your Citadel Miniatures is as much a personalised experience as collecting and gaming. Within the pages of this battletome and beyond, you will see many colour schemes that, should you choose to, you can copy in order to have your

Kharadron Overlords hail from a specific sky-port. On the other hand, perhaps you would prefer to use your own palette and paint your models in colours that appeal to you. Some painters enjoy lavishing hours of attention upon every model, bringing them up to the most spectacular individual standard they can manage. Others prefer to paint their models in batches, aiming to turn out entire regiments ready for battle whose coherent colour scheme and massed numbers make them look fantastic upon the tabletop. As with all aspects of this hobby, there's really no right or wrong way to do things so long as you're happy with the end result. So whether you're looking to assemble a battle-scarred

squadron of Arkanaut privateers, or the full majesty of a Kharadron fleet, embrace your creativity and get some paint on your brush!

WARHAMMER TV

Warhammer TV's painting tutorials have insights for everyone, as they show you how to paint Citadel Miniatures from start to finish. The guides are available for free on games-workshop.com, and can also be watched via the Warhammer TV YouTube channel. Why not take a moment to check them out?

SKYVESSEL HULL SCRATCHES

1 This hull has been painted with broad stripes of Thunderhawk Blue and Zamesi Desert. To add scratches, paint dashes of Russ Grey on the blue areas and Ushabti Bone on the yellow areas.

2 For a sharper effect, apply highlights of Administratum Grey onto the Russ Grey dashes and Pallid Wych Flesh onto the Ushabti Bone dashes.

3 Create the illusion of a recess by applying a line just above the upper edge of each dash. Use Rhinox Hide on the blue areas and Mournfang Brown on the yellow areas.

4 Finally, use Skrag Brown to simulate dribbles of rust and oil seeping from the cracks and the panels. For best results, we recommend using a fine brush such as an S Artificer Layer Brush.

COMPASSES FLEET SYMBOL

1

2

3

4

1 Paint a circle with two diagonal lines coming off it. You can use the hull's rivets as points of reference.

2 Now, paint a smaller circle within the first and add further lines to form thin triangles pointing away from it.

3 Fill in the shape you have just sketched out, forming the appearance of a pair of compasses.

4 With an XS Artificer Layer Brush, carefully add small navigational runes around the main symbol.

CROSS-AXE VESSEL SYMBOL

1

2

3

4

1 First, make sure you have achieved a smooth, flat underlying colour – in this case, Khorne Red.

2 Start by painting a simple cross of Averland Sunset. This acts as a basis for the rest of the symbol.

3 Next, add a line joining the bottom of the cross, and two thinner lines as a basis for the axe heads.

4 Fill out the shape of the axe heads by adding small triangles, cutting in with the base paint if necessary.

PORTHOLES

1

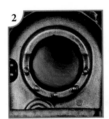
2

3

4

5

1 First, carefully basecoat the porthole with Abaddon Black.

2 Apply a layer of Warpstone Glow, leaving a small area of black at the top.

3 Now, paint a crescent of Moot Green around the bottom edge.

4 Next, paint an even thinner crescent of Yriel Yellow to outline the shape.

5 Lastly, apply Waystone Green to the entire area to give it a gloss sheen.

PORTHOLES USING TECHNICAL PAINTS

Top Tip: Using a gold basecoat instead of silver at this stage will slightly alter the hue of the following Technical paints – a silver basecoat is better if you want to maintain the paint's original colour.

Start with a basecoat of Leadbelcher – two thin coats works best.

Soulstone Blue painted over Leadbelcher gives a cold effect.

A Leadbelcher base emphasises the blue pigment in Waystone Green.

Spiritstone Red painted over Leadbelcher looks quite menacing.

BARAK-NAR

The warriors of Barak-Nar, City of the First Sunrise, wear overalls of regal purple underneath cold steel armour with gold flourishes.

Undercoat: Chaos Black Spray

Basecoat Stage: Leadbelcher, Screamer Pink, Zandri Dust (gloves and straps), Rakarth Flesh (rag), Balthasar Gold, Abaddon Black

BARAK-ZILFIN

The Windmasters of Barak-Zilfin complement their tempest-blue undersuits with warm bronze for an effective contrast.

Undercoat: Chaos Black Spray

Basecoat Stage: Leadbelcher, Balthasar Gold, Abaddon Black, The Fang, Rakarth Flesh, Rhinox Hide, Screamer Pink

BARAK-ZON

A militaristic sky-port, the proud warriors of Barak-Zon stand tall in their distinctive uniforms of red and deep blue.

Undercoat: Chaos Black Spray

Basecoat Stage: Khorne Red, Stegadon Scale Green (overalls), Retributor Armour (gold), Zandri Dust (straps), Leadbelcher (silver)

3

Shade Stage: Drakenhof Nightshade (armour), Nuln Oil Gloss (weapons), Druchii Violet (overalls), Seraphim Sepia, Agrax Earthshade Gloss (gold)

4

Layer 1 Stage: Ironbreaker, Fulgurite Copper, Genestealer Purple, Karak Stone (straps), Pallid Wych Flesh (rag), Dark Reaper (black)

5

Layer 2 Stage: Stormhost Silver (all metallics), Slaanesh Grey (overalls), Screaming Skull (straps), Fenrisian Grey (black)

3

Layer 1 Stage: Fulgurite Copper, Thunderhawk Blue, Mechanicus Standard Grey, Pallid Wych Flesh, Skrag Brown

4

Shade Stage: Reikland Fleshshade Gloss (bronze), Nuln Oil (overalls and steel), Druchii Violet (haft), Reikland Fleshshade (helm)

5

Layer 2 Stage: Sycorax Bronze, Russ Grey (overalls), White Scar (helm), Balor Brown, Administratum Grey, Stormhost Silver, Pink Horror

3

Shade Stage: Nuln Oil (armour and overalls), Reikland Fleshshade (gold), Nuln Oil, Nuln Oil Gloss (silver), Seraphim Sepia (straps)

4

Layer 1 Stage: Evil Sunz Scarlet, Auric Armour Gold, Sotek Green (overalls), Ushabti Bone (straps), Mechanicus Standard Grey (black)

5

Layer 2 Stage: Fire Dragon Bright (armour), Stormhost Silver (all metallics), Karak Stone (overalls), Administratum Grey (black)

BARAK-URBAZ

The profiteers of Barak-Urbaz are distinguished by pink-purple overalls and steel armour with a distinctive blue-green tint.

Undercoat: Chaos Black Spray

Basecoat Stage: Leadbelcher (silver), Balthasar Gold (light bronze), Screamer Pink (overalls), Mournfang Brown, Warplock Bronze (dark bronze)

BARAK-MHORNAR

Dark blue armour is the hallmark of Barak-Mhornar, a sky-port infamous for its dubious interpretation of the Kharadron Code.

Undercoat: Chaos Black Spray

Basecoat Stage: Leadbelcher (silver), Stegadon Scale Green (armour), Zandri Dust (overalls), Balthasar Gold (bronze), Rhinox Hide (leather)

BARAK-THRYNG

Not ones for ostentation, Arkanauts of Barak-Thryng wear a utilitarian beige plate over red overalls. Their ancestor icons are highly polished out of respect.

Undercoat: Corax White Spray

Basecoat Stage: Screaming Skull, Fulgurite Copper, Rhinox Hide, Leadbelcher, Abaddon Black, Khorne Red

3

4

5

Shade Stage: Nuln Oil Gloss (silver), Nuln Oil (overalls), Coelia Greenshade (armour), Agrax Earthshade (leather), Reikland Fleshshade (bronze)

Layer 1 Stage: Fulgurite Copper (bronze), Pink Horror (overalls), Skrag Brown (leather), Mechanicus Standard Grey (black)

Layer 2 Stage: Stormhost Silver (all metallics), Karak Stone (overalls), Balor Brown (leather), Administratum Grey (black)

3

4

5

Shade Stage: Nuln Oil (armour), Seraphim Sepia (overalls), Reikland Fleshshade Gloss (bronze), Nuln Oil Gloss (silver)

Layer 1 Stage: Sotek Green (armour), Ushabti Bone (overalls), Fulgurite Copper (bronze), Eshin Grey (black), Skrag Brown (leather)

Layer 2 Stage: Fenrisian Grey (armour), Pallid Wych Flesh (overalls), Administratum Grey (black), Stormhost Silver (all metallics)

3

4

5

Shade Stage: Seraphim Sepia (armour), Reikland Fleshshade Gloss (brass), Nuln Oil Gloss (silver), Nuln Oil (overalls)

Layer 1 Stage: Screaming Skull (armour), Stormhost Silver (all metallics), Dark Reaper (black), Evil Sunz Scarlet, Skrag Brown

Layer 2 Stage: White Scar (armour), Administratum Grey (black), Fire Dragon Bright (overalls), Balor Brown

ARKANAUT ADMIRAL KITBASH

1

First, take an Arkanaut Admiral armed with a Skalfhammer.

2

Using a Citadel Knife, cut off the hammer's flat face with care.

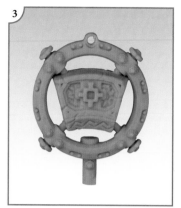

3

Use a Grundstok Thunderer Honour Bearer's standard for the next step.

4

Taking great care, cut out the runic stone from the ring of the standard.

5

Trim away the bottom section of the stone using the lowest line as a guide.

6

Now, attach the stone to the trimmed hammer to form a unique weapon.

PAINTING KHARADRON ARTEFACTS

1

Basecoat Stage: Leadbelcher, Retributor Armour (gold), Mechanicus Standard Grey, Warplock Bronze, Screamer Pink

2

Shade Stage: Nuln Oil Gloss (silver), Reikland Fleshshade Gloss (gold), Nuln Oil (head and haft)

3

Layer 1 Stage: Auric Armour Gold, Dawnstone (head), Pink Horror, White Scar (glow)

4

Layer 2 Stage: Stormhost Silver (all metallics), Administratum Grey (head), Emperor's Children (haft), Soulstone Blue (glow)

SKYWARDEN SUB-ASSEMBLY

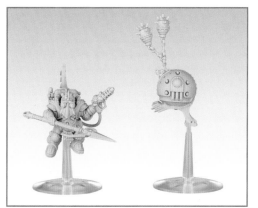

Instead of gluing the parts together, we left this Skywarden in two separate pieces – the duardin himself was mounted on a spare flying stand, and his aether-endrin on another.

The aether-endrin was undercoated with Retributor Armour Spray…

…while the Skywarden himself was undercoated with Chaos Black Spray.

BASES – PAINTING DIFFERENT ENVIRONMENTS

The masonry was painted Kantor Blue and Retributor Armour. These were all given a shade of Nuln Oil. Stirland Mud was applied to the base and when it was dry it was given a drybrush of Skrag Brown. The whole base was drybrushed Screaming Skull and Middenland Tufts were applied.

Here, the stone was painted using Stormvermin Fur and the brass embossed detail was given a basecoat of Warplock Bronze. The earth was painted with Astrogranite Debris and then drybrushed with Longbeard Grey. Finally, Valhallan Blizzard was added in patches for the snow.

This red-desert effect was achieved with Martian Ironcrust Technical paint drybrushed with Eldar Flesh. The masonry was painted with Stormvermin Fur and Retributor Armour.

This example uses Stirland Battlemire with a drybrushing of Dawnstone. The masonry was painted with Zandri Dust and Fulgurite Copper, and Mordheim Turf was used for the grass.

FORCES OF THE KHARADRON

This battletome contains all of the rules you need to field your Kharadron Overlords miniatures on the battlefields of the Mortal Realms, from a host of exciting allegiance abilities to a range of warscrolls and warscroll battalions. The rules are split into the following sections.

ALLEGIANCE ABILITIES

This section describes the allegiance abilities available to a Kharadron Overlords army. The rules for using allegiance abilities can be found in the *Warhammer Age of Sigmar Core Book*.

BATTLE TRAITS

Abilities available to units in a Kharadron Overlords army (pg 61).

COMMAND TRAITS

Abilities available to the general of a Kharadron Overlords army if it is a **Hero** (pg 62-63).

ARTEFACTS OF POWER

Artefacts available to **Heroes** in a Kharadron Overlords army (pg 64-65).

GREAT ENDRINWORKS

Special modifications available to **Skyvessels** in a Kharadron Overlords army (pg 66-67).

SKY-PORTS

Abilities for the six most famous Kharadron Overlords Sky-ports (pg 68-73). These rules can be used by units in a Kharadron Overlords army that have been given the appropriate keyword (see the Sky-ports battle trait, opposite).

BATTLEPLANS

This section includes a battleplan that can be played with a Kharadron Overlords army (pg 74-75).

PATH TO GLORY

This section contains rules for using your Kharadron Overlords collection in Path to Glory campaigns (pg 76-79).

WARSCROLLS

This section includes all of the warscrolls you will need to play games of Warhammer Age of Sigmar with your Kharadron Overlords miniatures.

There are three types of warscroll included in this section:

WARSCROLL BATTALIONS

These are formations made up of several Kharadron Overlords units that combine their strengths to gain powerful new abilities (pg 80-81).

WARSCROLLS

A warscroll for each unit is included here. The rules for using a Kharadron Overlords unit, along with its characteristics and abilities, are detailed on its warscroll (pg 82-95).

PITCHED BATTLE PROFILES

This section contains Pitched Battle profiles for the units and warscroll battalions in this book (pg 96).

ALLIES

This section also contains a list of the allies a Kharadron Overlords army can include (pg 96).

ALLEGIANCE ABILITIES
BATTLE TRAITS

MASTERS OF THE SKIES

SKY-PORTS

From the martial prospectors of Barak-Zon to the piratical raiders of Barak-Mhornar, the duardin of the different sky-ports are highly distinct in their character.

If your army is a Kharadron Overlords army, you can give it a Sky-port keyword from the list below instead of picking an artycle, amendment and footnote for your army. All **KHARADRON OVERLORDS** units in your army gain that keyword, and you must use the extra abilities listed for that Sky-port on the page indicated.

- **BARAK-NAR** (pg 68)
- **BARAK-ZILFIN** (pg 69)
- **BARAK-ZON** (pg 70)
- **BARAK-URBAZ** (pg 71)
- **BARAK-MHORNAR** (pg 72)
- **BARAK-THRYNG** (pg 73)

If a model already has a Sky-port keyword on its warscroll, it cannot gain another one. This does not preclude you from including the unit in your army.

AETHER-GOLD

Aether-gold is the lifeblood of Kharadron society, for this lighter-than-air metal holds their cities aloft, fuels their ships and powers a great deal of their weaponry.

Each **KHARADRON OVERLORDS HERO**, **SKYVESSEL** and **KHARADRON OVERLORDS** unit with 10 or more models starts a battle with 1 share of aether-gold.

Once per phase, you can say that 1 unit from your army that has any shares of aether-gold will spend 1 of them. If you do so, subtract 1 from that unit's Bravery characteristic for the rest of the battle, but you can pick a triumph it is eligible to use and immediately apply its effect to that unit. Ignore any restrictions on a triumph that say it can only be used once per battle if you pay to use it with a share of aether-gold.

STICK TO THE CODE
The Code guides every aspect of the Kharadron's lives.

When you choose a Kharadron Overlords army, you can pick 1 artycle, 1 amendment and 1 footnote for your army from the tables below. Alternatively, you can roll a D3 on each table to determine your army's interpretation of the Kharadron Code.

Artycle Table

D3	Artycle
1	**Honour is Everything:** You can re-roll hit rolls of 1 for attacks made by friendly **KHARADRON OVERLORDS HEROES** that target a **HERO** or **MONSTER**.
2	**Master the Skies:** You can re-roll hit rolls of 1 for attacks made by friendly **SKYVESSELS** that target a unit that can fly.
3	**Settle the Grudges:** After armies are set up but before the first battle round begins, pick 1 enemy unit. You can re-roll hit rolls of 1 for attacks made by friendly **KHARADRON OVERLORDS** units that target that unit.

Amendment Table

D3	Amendment
1	**Always Take What You Are Owed:** Pick up to D3 different **KHARADRON OVERLORDS** units in your army. Each of those units starts the battle with 1 share of aether-gold in addition to any they normally receive.
2	**Prosecute Wars With All Haste:** In your first turn, friendly **KHARADRON OVERLORDS** units can run and still shoot later in the turn.
3	**Trust To Your Guns:** Add 1 to the Bravery characteristic of friendly **KHARADRON OVERLORDS** units while they are more than 3" from any enemy units.

Footnote Table

D3	Footnote
1	**There's No Reward Without Risk:** Once per battle, you can re-roll a charge roll for a friendly **KHARADRON OVERLORDS** unit.
2	**There's No Trading With Some People:** Once per battle, a friendly **KHARADRON OVERLORDS** unit that has run and/or retreated in the same turn can still shoot and/or charge.
3	**Without Our Ships, We Are Naught:** Once per battle, you can heal up to D3 wounds allocated to a friendly **SKYVESSEL**.

COMMAND TRAITS

LORDS OF THE SKY-FLEETS
Arkanaut Admiral only.

D6 Command Trait

1 Wealthy: *This mighty champion has built up a vast fortune during his lucrative career.*

This general starts the battle with 2 shares of aether-gold instead of 1.

2 Tough as Old Boots: *This renowned officer is amongst the hardiest of their kind.*

Add 2 to this general's Wounds characteristic.

3 Grudgebearer: *This leader never forgets a slight, biding their time until they can take revenge!*

After armies are set up, pick 1 enemy **Hero**. Double the damage inflicted by weapons used by this general that target that **Hero**.

4 Cunning Fleetmaster: *This wily admiral never does what the enemy expects.*

After armies are set up, but before the first battle round begins, you can make a normal move with 1 friendly **Skyvessel**. It can fly high unless it is an **Arkanaut Ironclad**.

5 War Wound: *This general's famous battle wisdom has been painfully learnt.*

Roll a dice for this general in your hero phase. On a 1, subtract 1 from hit rolls for this general until your next hero phase. On a 2+, you receive 1 command point.

6 A Scholar and an Arkanaut: *This general's knowledge of the Kharadron code is unrivalled.*

You can pick an extra footnote for your army. You cannot pick a footnote your army already has.

SENIOR ENDRINEERS
Endrinmaster only.

D6 Command Trait

1 Wealthy: *This mighty champion has built up a vast fortune during his lucrative career.*

This general starts the battle with 2 shares of aether-gold instead of 1.

2 Tough as Old Boots: *This renowned officer is amongst the hardiest of their kind.*

Add 2 to this general's Wounds characteristic.

3 Grudgebearer: *This leader never forgets a slight, biding their time until they can take revenge!*

After armies are set up, pick 1 enemy **Hero**. Double the damage inflicted by weapons used by this general that target that **Hero**.

4 Grandmaster: *This Endrinmaster's knowledge of the intricacies of Kharadron skyvessel design is unmatched.*

When you use this general's Endrinmaster ability, add 1 to the number of wounds the ability allows you to heal.

5 Great Tinkerer: *This famed inventor is always coming up with ways to improve their creations.*

Add 2 to the Attacks characteristic of this general's Gaze of Grungni weapon.

6 Endrinprofessor: *This cantankerous scholar expects perfection from their students.*

Once in each of your hero phases, this general can use the By Grungni, I Have My Eye On You! command ability without a command point being spent.

READERS OF THE GUIDING WINDS
AETHERIC NAVIGATOR only.

D6   Command Trait

1   Wealthy: *This mighty champion has built up a vast fortune during his lucrative career.*

This general starts the battle with 2 shares of aether-gold instead of 1.

2   Tough as Old Boots: *This renowned officer is amongst the hardiest of their kind.*

Add 2 to this general's Wounds characteristic.

3   Stormcaller: *This brilliant Navigator guides aetheric zephyrs as a maestro conducts an orchestra.*

When this general uses their Aetherstorm ability, you can re-roll the dice that determines what effect it has on the enemy unit.

4   Ride the Winds: *Nobody can read the wind currents more accurately than this Aetheric Navigator.*

Add 3" to the Move characteristic of a **SKYVESSEL** that has this general in its garrison.

5   Sceptic: *This stubborn Navigator refuses to believe that magic is anything but superstition.*

Add 1 to dispelling and unbinding rolls for this general.

6   Diviner: *This Navigator can use their aethersight to help determine in advance where deposits of aether-gold will be found.*

After armies are set up, pick 1 terrain feature or objective. Do not take battleshock tests for friendly **KHARADRON OVERLORDS** units while they are wholly within 12" of that terrain feature or objective.

ALCHEMICAL INNOVATORS
AETHER-KHEMIST only.

D6   Command Trait

1   Wealthy: *This mighty champion has built up a vast fortune during his lucrative career.*

This general starts the battle with 2 shares of aether-gold instead of 1.

2   Tough as Old Boots: *This renowned officer is amongst the hardiest of their kind.*

Add 2 to this general's Wounds characteristic.

3   Grudgebearer: *This leader never forgets a slight, biding their time until they can take revenge!*

After armies are set up, pick 1 enemy **HERO**. Double the damage inflicted by weapons used by this general that target that **HERO**.

4   A Nose for Gold: *This Aether-Khemist's finely honed senses lead them unerringly to hidden deposits of aether-gold.*

Roll a dice for this general in your hero phase. On a 5+, they gain 1 share of aether-gold.

5   Genius in the Making: *This Aether-Khemist is already renowned, even though they are a mere stripling only a few dozen seasons old.*

The range of this general's Aetheric Augmentation ability is 18" instead of 12".

6   Collector: *This Aether-Khemist spends most of their aether-gold on the acquisition of rare and powerful artefacts.*

If you choose this general to have an artefact of power, you can choose 1 extra friendly **HERO** to have an artefact of power.

ARTEFACTS OF POWER

PERKS OF RANK
ARKANAUT ADMIRAL only.

D6   Artefact of Power

1   **Masterwrought Armour:** *This finely wrought and detailed suit of armour is the acme of the armourer's art.*

Roll a dice each time you allocate a wound or mortal wound to the bearer. On a 6, that wound or mortal wound is negated.

2   **Hammer of Aetheric Might:** *When swung with enough force, this weapon can release its supercharged aether-energies in a brilliant flash.*

Pick 1 of the bearer's melee weapons. If the unmodified hit roll for an attack made with that weapon is 6, that attack inflicts 1 mortal wound on the target in addition to its normal damage.

3   **Gattleson's Endless Repeater:** *Named after its famous inventor, this gun houses an aether-supercharger that gives it a tremendous rate of fire.*

Add 2 to the Attacks characteristic of the bearer's Volley Pistol.

4   **Rune of Mark:** *Upon this document is scribed the name of a hated foe; should that foe be slain, the bearer will be richly rewarded.*

After armies are set up, pick 1 enemy **HERO**. If that **HERO** is slain, before the model is removed from play you can give 1 share of aether-gold each to the 3 closest friendly **KHARADRON OVERLORDS** units to that **HERO**.

5   **Flask of Vintage Amberwhisky:** *This rare duardin drink is said to be good for whatever ails you.*

Once per battle, in your hero phase, you can either heal up to D6 wounds allocated to the bearer or heal up to 2 wounds allocated to the bearer.

6   **Proclamator Mask-hailer:** *Not even the hardest of hearing can fail to understand any commands issued through a Proclamator Mask-hailer.*

Once per battle round, this general can use a command ability on their warscroll without a command point being spent.

AETHERMATIC INSTRUMENTS
AETHERIC NAVIGATOR only.

D3   Artefact of Power

1   **Cyclonic Aethometer:** *This intricate device adds to the fury of any aetherstorm that its bearer creates.*

When you use the bearer's Aetherstorm ability, add 1 to the dice roll that determines its effect.

2   **Svaregg-Stein 'Illuminator' Flarepistol:** *This highly prized ranging pistol lights up its mark, making it an easy target for other skyfarers and vessels that shoot at it.*

The first time in a battle that the bearer's Ranging Pistol scores a hit on an enemy unit, you can re-roll hit rolls for attacks made by other friendly **KHARADRON OVERLORDS** units that target that enemy unit in the same phase.

3   **Voidstone Orb:** *This small, unassuming black globe contains the power to disrupt spells that an enemy might try to cast.*

Once per battle, when you use the bearer's Aethersight ability, you can say that the bearer will use their Voidstone Orb. If you do so, the dispelling or unbinding roll for that use of the ability is automatically successful (do not roll the dice).

INGENIOUS GADGETS
Endrinmaster only.

Endrinmaster with Endrinharness

D3   Artefact of Power

1   Cogmonculus: *This small cogwork automaton keeps the Endrinmaster's equipment in perfect working order.*

Once per phase, you can re-roll 1 hit or wound roll for an attack made by the bearer, or re-roll 1 save roll for an attack that targets the bearer. You cannot use this ability to re-roll more than 1 dice per phase.

2   Aetherquartz Monolens: *This expertly crafted crystal lens greatly increases the range of any Gaze of Grungni projector it is attached to.*

The bearer's Gaze of Grungni has a Range of 18" instead of 9".

3   Seismic Shock-gauntlets: *When the bearer moves swiftly, these kinetically powered gauntlets gather large amounts of energy that can be unleashed upon contact with the foe.*

After the bearer makes a charge move, you can pick 1 enemy unit within 1" of the bearer and roll a dice. On a 2+, that enemy unit suffers D3 mortal wounds.

Endrinmaster with Dirigible Suit

D3   Artefact of Power

1   Aether-injection Boosters: *These powerful boot-jets allow the wearer to quickly escape from combat.*

When the bearer retreats, they can use the Disengage and Fly High abilities from the Grundstok Gunhauler warscroll (pg 92).

2   Phosphorite Bomblets: *When these grenades explode, they scatter blazing phosphorite all around that burns with a white-hot heat.*

Once per battle, in your shooting phase, you can pick 1 unit within 6" of this model and roll a dice. On a 2+, that unit suffers 1 mortal wound you can roll again. Keep on rolling until the target is destroyed or you roll a 1.

3   Miniaturised Aethermatic Repulsion Field: *This small device pushes arcane energies away from the one who carries it.*

Each time the bearer is affected by a spell or endless spell, you can roll a dice. If you do so, on a 3+, ignore the effects of that spell on the bearer.

AETHER-GOLD INVENTIONS
Aether-Khemist only.

D3   Artefact of Power

1   Emergency Ventplates: *When these vents are triggered they belch forth an opaque cloud of harmless vapour that hides the Aether-Khemist from sight.*

Once per battle, at the start of the enemy shooting phase, you can say that the bearer will use their Emergency Ventplates. If you do so, subtract 1 from hit rolls for attacks that target the bearer or any friendly unit wholly within 6" of the bearer.

2   Caustic Anatomiser: *When special gas canisters in this anatomiser are triggered, the bearer is surrounded by a dense cloud of deadly corrosive gas.*

Once per battle, at the start of the combat phase, you can say that the bearer will use their Caustic Anatomiser. If you do so, roll a dice for each enemy model within 6" of this model. For each 5+, that model's unit suffers 1 mortal wound.

3   Spell in a Bottle: *This Aether-Khemist has used the alchemical arts to transmute an endless spell into an inert gas and trap it in a carefully crafted container. When the container is shattered, the endless spell is freed.*

Pick 1 endless spell. Any endless spell can be chosen (all restrictions are ignored) but you must pay any points required for the model. Once per battle, the bearer can automatically cast that endless spell (do not roll 2D6) and it cannot be unbound.

GREAT ENDRINWORKS

If a Kharadron Overlords army includes any **SKYVESSELS**, 1 of those **SKYVESSELS** can have a great endrinwork. Declare which **SKYVESSEL** has the great endrinwork and then pick which great endrinwork table you wish to use. You can choose or roll for a great endrinwork from the table you pick. You can choose 1 extra **SKYVESSEL** to have a great endrinwork for each warscroll battalion in your army. A **SKYVESSEL** cannot have more than 1 great endrinwork, and an army may not include duplicates of the same great endrinwork.

IRONCLAD MAJOR INSTALLATIONS
ARKANAUT IRONCLAD only.

D6   **Great Endrinwork**

1   **The Last Word:** *When all seems lost, this vessel's greatest weapon continues to thunder.*

At the end of the enemy charge phase you can pick 1 enemy unit that finished a charge move in that phase within 3" of this model. This model can shoot at that unit with its Great Sky Cannon, Great Skyhook or Great Volley Cannon.

2   **Hegsson Solutions 'Old Reliable' Hullplates:** *These hullplates are renowned for their ability to absorb damage without failing.*

Add 2 to this model's Wounds characteristic.

3   **Ebullient Buoyancy Aid:** *This aether-enhancing unit increases the buoyancy of even the largest ships, making it particularly useful in thin atmospheres.*

This model can fly high and/or disengage even while it has a garrison of 16 or more models.

4   **Prudency Chutes:** *These reliable safety devices allow passengers to safely evacuate a crippled skyvessel.*

If this model is destroyed, you do not have to roll to see if models in its garrison are slain (they all survive).

5   **Magnificent Omniscope:** *This apparatus makes the winds aetheric clearly visible to the ship's Navigator.*

Add 2" to this model's Move characteristic.

6   **Zonbarcorp 'Dealbreaker' Battle Ram:** *The Dealbreaker is a large battering ram that smashes opponents to the ground.*

After this model makes a charge move, you can pick 1 enemy unit within 1" of this model, and roll a number of dice equal to the charge roll for that charge move. For each 4+, that enemy unit suffers 1 mortal wound.

FRIGATE REFITTINGS
ARKANAUT FRIGATE only.

D3   **Great Endrinwork**

1   **Magnificent Omniscope:** *This apparatus makes the winds aetheric clearly visible to the ship's Navigator.*

Add 2" to this model's Move characteristic.

2   **Prudency Chutes:** *These reliable safety devices allow passengers to safely evacuate a crippled skyvessel.*

If this skyvessel is destroyed, you do not have to roll to see if models in its garrison are slain (they all survive).

3   **Malefic Skymines:** *Invented during the Great Harpy Migrations, these mines pack a mean punch.*

Once per battle, at the start of the combat phase, you can pick 1 enemy unit that can fly and is within 6" of this model and roll a dice. On a 2-3, that enemy unit suffers D3 mortal wounds. On a 4+, that enemy unit suffers D6 mortal wounds.

GUNHAULER MODIFICATIONS
Grundstok Gunhauler only.

D3   Great Endrinwork

1   Iggrind-Kaz Surge-injection Endrin Mk. IV: *This skyvessel's endrinsphere lets its Captain boost it across the skies, though at the risk of the endrinsphere overheating.*

When this model makes a normal move, you can add D3" to that move. If you wish, you can add 2D3" to that move instead of D3", but if you do so and you roll a double, then this model suffers 1 mortal wound after the move is made.

2   Zonbarcorp 'Debtsettler' Spar Torpedo: *A powerful torpedo is mounted to the front of this skyvessel at the end of a sturdy spar. When the warhead strikes an object, it explodes with devastating force.*

Once per battle, after this model makes its first charge move, you can pick 1 enemy unit within 1" of this model and roll a dice. On a 2+, that enemy unit suffers D6 mortal wounds.

3   Coalbeard's Collapsible Compartments: *This Gunhauler is fitted with small compartments that allow it to carry passengers.*

This model can use the Flying Transport ability from the Arkanaut Ironclad warscroll (pg 90). If it does so, the maximum number of models that can garrison it is 5 instead of 25, and it can always fly high and/or disengage no matter how many models are in its garrison.

BARAK-NAR, CITY OF THE FIRST SUNRISE

The brightest jewel in the Kharadron empire is the sky-port of Barak-Nar. A titan of cutting-edge science and industry, the City of the First Sunrise can boast more airfleets than any of its rivals, each commanded by an intrepid officer armed to the teeth with the latest aethermatic weaponry.

Though the City of the First Sunrise suffered greatly during the Garaktormun, it remains the most potent symbol of Kharadron might. Possessing the guiding hand on the Geldraad and a greater vault of riches than any other sky-port, Barak-Nar's quest for supremacy has only escalated in the years following that catastrophe. With every dawn, dozens of intrepid airship commanders launch voyages into wild, new lands in search of undiscovered aether-gold streams.

As befitting the sky-port's status as the foremost centre of scientific innovation in the empire , Barak-Nar officers deploy cutting-edge aethermatic inventions and weapons with devastating effectiveness in the search for profit. For these confident duardin, ingenuity trumps brute force every time, and their unflappable belief in the march of progress is an inspiration to the privateers under their command – particularly in this age of rogue arcane phenomena. With the aid of Barak-Nar's superlative guild technicians, such hazards are easily dealt with; enemy spells are rendered inert with a precise application of ultra-refined ather-gold, while a pinpoint cannonade from the sky-port's heavy ships of the line takes care of any remaining threats.

ABILITIES
Scholars and Commanders: *The leaders of Barak-Nar embrace the laws of science, using the knowledge they have gained to help defeat their foes.*

At the start of the first battle round, roll a dice for each friendly **BARAK-NAR HERO** on the battlefield (including any that are part of a garrison). For each 4+, you receive 1 extra command point.

KHARADRON CODE
Your army must use the following interpretation of the Kharadron Code:

Artycle – Respect Your Commanders: You can re-roll battleshock tests for friendly **BARAK-NAR** units while they are wholly within 12" of a friendly **BARAK-NAR HERO**.

Amendment – Trust Aethermatics, Not Superstition: Each **BARAK-NAR HERO** can attempt to unbind 1 spell in the enemy hero phase. If they can already attempt to unbind a spell, they can attempt to unbind 1 extra spell in the enemy hero phase.

Footnote – Through Knowledge, Power: Add 1 to unbinding rolls for **BARAK-NAR HEROES**.

COMMAND TRAIT
A **BARAK-NAR** general must have this command trait instead of one listed on pages 62-63:

Champion of Progress: *Barak-Nar is at the very forefront of the Kharadron Overlords' advance, and the confidence of their leaders is palpable.*

Do not take battleshock for friendly **BARAK-NAR** units while they are wholly within 12" of this general.

ARTEFACT OF POWER
The first **BARAK-NAR HERO** to receive an artefact of power must be given an Aethercharged Rune:

Aethercharged Rune: *This rune is infused with a glowing charge of aether-power, which can be drawn upon by its bearer when the need arises.*

Once per battle you can change either 1 hit roll for an attack made by the bearer or 1 save roll for an attack that targets the bearer to the roll of your choice.

BARAK-ZILFIN, THE WINDSWEPT CITY

There are no finer aeronautical sailors than those out of Barak-Zilfin, as they themselves are only too happy to point out. On countless occasions the skilful manoeuvres and breathtaking speed of the sky-port's elite airfleets have carried the day against seemingly impossible odds.

The duardin of Barak-Zilfin are known as the 'Windmasters' – an apt moniker, for none can anticipate and ride the Mortal Realms' air currents quite as skilfully as they. Time and again the sky-port's fleets have managed to outmanoeuvre and outpace their rivals, winning the race to secure lucrative aether-gold fields and add to their considerable profits. Such is the reverence that Barak-Zilfin crew hold for their vessels, that they will patch up any damage done to their ships before even thinking about attending to their own wounds.

The master shipwrights of the Windswept City are famed for their meticulous craftsmanship. Though the scale of production in Barak-Zilfin cannot match the industry of Barak-Nar, the vessels produced by the sky-port's Great Coghalls are accepted by most Kharadron as the finest of their kind. Each is a custom-crafted marvel, fitted with the most advanced endrinthrusters and streamlined hull profiles, designed to fly rings around enemy craft. In the hands of an expert commander, such vessels are all but uncatchable, capable of pulling off breathtaking aeronautical manoeuvres that would tear any other sky-ship apart at the rivets.

ABILITIES
Magnificent Skyvessels: *The skyvessels of the Barak-Zilfin fleets are second to none.*

You can choose 1 extra **Skyvessel** in your army to have a great endrinwork.

KHARADRON CODE
Your army must use the following interpretation of the Kharadron Code:

Artycle – Master the Skies: You can re-roll hit rolls of 1 for attacks made by friendly **Skyvessels** that target a unit that can fly.

Amendment – Don't Argue With the Wind: In your movement phase, if you declare a friendly **Barak-Zilfin** unit will run, do not make a run roll. Instead, add 6" to the Move characteristic of all models in that unit for that phase.

Footnote – There's Always a Breeze If You Look For It: Once per battle, in your hero phase, 1 friendly **Barak-Zilfin** unit can make a normal move (it can run, retreat or disengage).

COMMAND TRAIT
A **Barak-Zilfin** general that is an **Arkanaut Admiral** must have this command trait instead of one listed on page 62:

Master Commander: *The Admirals of Barak-Zilfin read their fleets' movements with expert skill, reacting swiftly when opportunity presents itself.*

If this general is part of your army and on the battlefield, each time you spend a command point to use a command ability on this general's warscroll, roll a dice. On a 5+, you receive 1 extra command point.

ARTEFACT OF POWER
The first **Barak-Zilfin Hero** to receive an artefact of power must be given the Staff of Ocular Optimisation:

Staff of Ocular Optimisation: *Highly refined lenses and aether filters allow the owner of this device to accurately see through any murk.*

Pick 1 of the bearer's missile weapons. Add 1 to hit rolls for attacks made by that weapon.

BARAK-ZON, CITY OF THE SUN

Highly militaristic and prideful of their unrivalled martial heritage, Arkanauts of Barak-Zon long to prove themselves in battle and earn the famous Ironstar – a medal awarded only for acts of exceptional valour. There are no finer soldiers in all the sky-ports than those trained within the drillhouses of the City of the Sun.

Amongst their fellow sky-ports the folk of Barak-Zon are regarded as a warlike bunch, more concerned with combat honours and drilling than earning a respectable profit. Those of the City of the Sun care not a cog for the thoughts of envious rivals. They know well that aggressive negotiations obtain the greatest rewards. From an early age, all citizens of Barak-Zon are required to take part in daily shooting practice, and the sky-port's Musterpresses are notoriously demanding. This harsh training ensures that only the fiercest recruits earn a place in the city's Arkanaut companies.

While many of their rivals rely upon the sheer power of their ships to blast their foes into submission, the Admirals of Barak-Zon instead utilise the peerless marksmanship and sharp cutlasses of their elite infantry. Swift aerial deployments deliver these hardened soldiers to the heart of the battle, where their guns are brought to bear upon the enemy with deadly results. These formations are often led by veterans bearing the fabled Ironstar – the famed medal of honour granted only for actions of valorous distinction.

ABILITIES

Deeds, Not Words: *The martially minded warriors of Barak-Zon are famous for taking the fight straight to the foe, launching glorious charges that see them strike at the foe with great vigour.*

Add 1 to wound rolls for attacks made with melee weapons by friendly **Skyfarers** units that made a charge move in the same turn, and add 1 to hit rolls for attacks made with melee weapons by friendly **Skywardens** units that made a charge move in the same turn.

KHARADRON CODE

Your army must use the following interpretation of the Kharadron Code:

Artycle – Honour is Everything: You can re-roll hit rolls of 1 for attacks made by friendly **Barak-Zon Heroes** that target a **Hero** or **Monster**.

Amendment – Leave No Duardin Behind: Add 2 to the Bravery characteristic of friendly **Skyfarers** units while they are wholly within 12" of a friendly **Skyvessel**.

Footnote – Show Them Your Steel: Once per battle, in your hero phase, 1 friendly **Skyfarers** unit that is part of a garrison on a **Skyvessel** can leave that garrison. Set up that unit wholly within 3" of that **Skyvessel** and more than 9" from any enemy units.

COMMAND TRAIT

A **Barak-Zon** general must have this command trait instead of one listed on pages 62-63:

Bearer of the Ironstar: *The famed Ironstar of Barak-Zon is awarded only for feats of singular valour.*

The first time this general is slain, before removing them, roll a dice. On a 2+ they are not slain, you can heal up to D3 wounds allocated to them, and any wounds remaining to be allocated to them are negated.

ARTEFACT OF POWER

The first **Barak-Zon Hero** to receive an artefact of power must be given the Aethersped Hammer:

Aethersped Hammer: *This aethermatically enhanced hammer allows the user to strike again and again at ferocious speed.*

Pick 1 of the bearer's melee weapons. Add 2 to the Attacks characteristic of that weapon.

BARAK-URBAZ, THE MARKET CITY

Those of Barak-Urbaz are notorious even amongst the Kharadron for their ability to employ subtleties and technicalities in the Code for their own benefit. This officious attitude is exemplified by the sky-port's Aether-Khemists, who can wring more power from their alchemical compounds than any of their peers.

The Kharadron empire is founded upon the power of trade, and there are no wilier merchants than those of Barak-Urbaz. The sky-port's military commanders know the intricacies of the Kharadron Code inside out, and are experts at exploiting minor imprecisions and loopholes in the constitution for their own ends. They are single-mindedly ruthless in their pursuit of profit, ensuring that each voyage accumulates an impressive share of aether-gold by any means necessary.

Aether-Khemists of Barak-Urbaz are rightly regarded as the foremost practitioners of their craft. The sky-port's master alchemists have invented several innovative methods of extracting the maximum power and potential from every mote of Grungni's Breath. Thus, although the sky-port's aether-gold reserves cannot match the sheer volume of those of Barak-Nar or Barak-Zilfin, it remains a deceptively powerful player in Kharadron politics. Indeed, no other sky-port has successfully added so many amendments to the Code as Barak-Urbaz.

ABILITIES

The Market City: *Barak-Urbaz Codewrights can squeeze every last drop of profit from any situation.*

Do not subtract 1 from the Bravery characteristic of an **BARAK-URBAZ** unit that spends a share of aether-gold.

KHARADRON CODE

Your army must use the following interpretation of the Kharadron Code:

Artycle – Seek New Prospects: You can re-roll battleshock tests for friendly **BARAK-URBAZ** units while they are wholly within your opponent's territory.

Amendment – Always Take What You Are Owed: Pick up to D3 different friendly **BARAK-URBAZ** units. Each of those units starts the battle with 1 share of aether-gold in addition to any they normally receive.

Footnote – Where There's War, There's Gold: Once per battle, at the end of the combat phase, 1 friendly **SKYFARERS** unit that fought in that phase gains 1 share of aether-gold.

COMMAND TRAIT

A **BARAK-URBAZ** general that is an **AETHER-KHEMIST** must have this command trait instead of one listed on page 63:

Khemist Supreme: *The Aether-Khemists of Barak-Urbaz are paragons of their chemical-based craft.*

Replace the rules for this general's Aetheric Augmentation ability with: 'In your hero phase you can pick 2 friendly **SKYFARERS** units wholly within 12" of this model. Until your next hero phase, you can re-roll wound rolls of 1 for attacks made by those units. This ability cannot be used by an **AETHER-KHEMIST** that is part of a garrison, or on a friendly unit that is part of a garrison.'

GREAT ENDRINWORK

The first **BARAK-URBAZ SKYVESSEL** to receive a great endrinwork must be given the Breath of Morgrim:

Breath of Morgrim: *The prow of this skyvessel has been modified to belch forth great clouds of toxic gas.*

In your shooting phase, you can pick 1 enemy unit and roll 1 dice for each model from that unit within 6" of the bearer. For each 6, that unit suffers 1 mortal wound.

BARAK-MHORNAR, THE CITY OF SHADOW

What some call piracy, those of Barak-Mhornar simply view as clever opportunism. Always skirting the boundaries of accepted practice when it comes to matters of the Code, these duardin prefer to strike without warning, killing their quarry and stripping them of anything valuable before disappearing into the shadows.

Fleets out of the hidden sky-port of Barak-Mhornar have a well-earned reputation for cunning and deceit. By striking rapidly from unexpected quarters, the denizens of the City of Shadow have earned many stunning victories over their rivals. They employ every conceivable tactic in order to gain an advantage, such as bearing the colours of neutral sky-ports, launching pre-emptive strikes without any formal declaration of hostilities, and mining well-trafficked air lanes.

The fact that other Kharadron decry these underhanded tactics matters not at all to those of Barak-Mhornar, for they ensure that even their most cut-throat methods are excused – or at the very least omitted from mention – by the Kharadron Code. Due to this streak of ruthlessness, and despite its relatively modest armada, Barak-Mhornar is treated with wary concern by even the greatest sky-ports. Both Barak-Nar and Barak-Zon have devoted vast resources to uncovering the true location of the mysterious City of Shadow, thus far to no avail.

ABILITIES

Fearsome Raiders: *By attacking rapidly from unexpected quarters, the denizens of the City of Shadow strike fear in the hearts of their foes.*

Subtract 1 from the Bravery characteristic of enemy units while they are within 6" of any friendly **Barak-Mhornar** units.

KHARADRON CODE

Your army must use the following interpretation of the Kharadron Code:

Artycle – Seek New Prospects: You can re-roll battleshock tests for friendly **Barak-Mhornar** units while they are wholly within your opponent's territory.

Amendment – Prosecute Wars With All Haste: In your first turn, friendly **Barak-Mhornar** units can run and still shoot later in the turn.

Footnote – Who Strikes First, Strikes Hardest: Once per battle, at the start of your combat phase, you can pick 1 friendly **Barak-Mhornar** unit that is within 3" of an enemy unit. That friendly unit fights at the start of that combat phase, but cannot fight again in that combat phase unless an ability or spell allows it to fight more ᵗhan once.

COMMAND TRAIT

A **Barak-Mhornar** general must have this command trait instead of one listed on pages 62-63:

Opportunistic Privateer: *This feared buccaneer strikes swiftly and without warning, crushing their enemies before they have a chance to react.*

If this general is part of the garrison of a **Skyvessel** that is on is on the battlefield after armies are set up but before the first battle round begins, you can remove that **Skyvessel** from the battlefield and set it up again anywhere more than 9" from any enemy units. If you do so, that **Skyvessel** cannot make a normal move in the first battle round, and units in its garrison cannot leave the garrison in the first battle round.

ARTEFACT OF POWER

The first **Barak-Mhornar Navigator** to receive an artefact of power must be given the Galeforce Stave:

Galeforce Stave: *This mighty device can be used to direct great gusts of aetheric winds at a charging foe, slowing their charge down to a crawl.*

At the start of the enemy charge phase, you can pick 1 enemy unit within 12" of the bearer. Halve charge rolls for that unit in that phase.

BARAK-THRYNG, CITY OF THE ANCESTORS

Truculent, ill-tempered, stuck in the past and set in their ways: these are just a few terms used by rival sky-ports to describe those who hail from Barak-Thryng. These ultra-conservative duardin judge everything against the glories of the past, and inevitably find that it measures short.

All duardin have a tendency to maintain grudges and dwell upon perceived slights, but the dour traditionalists of Barak-Thryng take such things to another level entirely. Their resentments burn hot and fiercely for centuries, and they take great pleasure in ensuring that every insult is eventually repaid in kind. When a soldier of Barak-Thryng gets the opportunity to wreak revenge upon their enemies in battle, they will fight with single-minded stubbornness, refusing to even contemplate death until they have spilled their nemeses' blood.

At the heart of the City of the Ancestors lies the Grudgehall, where every offence against the sky-port is inscribed upon a rune-slate and added to a extensive library that covers an entire district. The sky-port's soldiers are encouraged to settle these grudges whenever possible, and often carry runic tablets listing the most grievous insults into battle, so that they may ensure that vengeance is properly delivered. It is said that this pleases the duardin gods – to whom the people of Barak-Thryng still pay tribute, more out of tradition than piety.

ABILITIES
Incredibly Stubborn: *The warriors of Barak-Thryng will often deny death long enough to get in a last blow.*

If a friendly **Skyfarers** model is slain while it is within 3" of an enemy unit, roll a dice. On a 4+, that model can fight before it is removed from play.

KHARADRON CODE
Your army must use the following interpretation of the Kharadron Code:

Artycle – Chronicle of Grudges: After armies are set up but before the first battle round begins, pick up to 3 different enemy units. You can re-roll hit rolls of 1 for attacks made by friendly **Barak-Thryng** units that target those units.

Amendment – Take Help Where You Can Get It: 1 in 4 units in your army can be a **Duardin** unit that does not have the **Kharadron Overlords** keyword. Those units gain the **Barak-Thryng** keyword. They cannot be the army general and do not count towards the number of Battleline units in the army.

Footnote – Honour the Gods, Just in Case: Once per battle, at the start of your shooting phase or a combat phase, you can pick 1 friendly **Barak-Thryng** unit.

Until the end of that phase, unmodified hit rolls of 6 for attacks made by that unit score 2 hits on the target instead of 1. Make a wound and save roll for each hit.

COMMAND TRAIT
A **Barak-Thryng** general must have this command trait instead of one listed on pages 62-63:

Supremely Stubborn: *This commander is notoriously stubborn, even for a lord of Barak-Thryng.*

When you use the Incredibly Stubborn ability for this general, they can fight on a roll of 2+ instead of 4+.

ARTEFACT OF POWER
The first **Barak-Thryng Skyfarer Hero** to receive an artefact of power must be given a Grudgehammer:

Grudgehammer: *These ancient and highly revered hammers are said to be especially deadly when they are used to settle long-remembered slights.*

Pick one of the bearer's melee weapons. Add 1 to hit rolls for attacks made by that weapon. In addition, if the unmodified wound roll for an attack made by that weapon that targets an enemy unit which was picked for the Chronicle of Grudges artycle is 6, that attack inflicts D3 mortal wounds on the target in addition to any normal damage.

BATTLEPLAN
PROSPECTORS DOWN!

The life of an Arkanaut is a dangerous one, and every duardin knows the risks of their profession. Many are the vessels that have been lost to mishap, monster or maelstrom, with no trace of their crews. Occasionally, however, the survivors of such an event manage to get a message back to their kin, and a rescue mission is launched with all haste. It becomes a race to recover the lost duardin – and their aether-gold – before anyone else discovers them.

This battleplan lets you stage a daring rescue with your force of Kharadron Overlords, even as the enemy bears down on the survivors, intent on their destruction.

THE ARMIES

Each player picks an army. One player is the Kharadron Overlords player. The other player is the Opportunist. The Kharadron Overlords player must use a Kharadron Overlords army, and it must include at least 1 unit that can fly and 1 unit that cannot fly.

CONTINGENTS

Once the Kharadron Overlords player has picked their army, they must split it into a survivors contingent and a rescuers contingent. Each contingent must have at least 1 unit. The survivors cannot include any units that can fly. The rescuers must all be able to fly, or arrive on the battlefield as part of the garrison of a rescuers unit that can fly.

The Kharadron Overlords player can pick 2 generals instead of 1. One general must be part of the survivors contingent, and 1 general must be part of the rescuers contingent.

THE BATTLEFIELD

The Kharadron player must first set up 1 terrain feature wholly within their territory. Set up the rest of the terrain as described in the core rules.

SET-UP

The Kharadron Overlords player sets up their survivors contingent first, wholly within their territory. The rescuers contingent starts the battle in reserve, and will arrive as described later.

The Opportunist then sets up their army wholly within their territory, more than 12" from enemy units. The territories are shown on the map below.

FIRST TURN

The Opportunist takes the first turn in the first battle round.

COMMAND ABILITIES

The following additional command abilities can be used in this battle.

Sell Your Lives Dearly: *The leader of the survivors knows that they are out of time, and they prepare to make the enemy pay.*

The Kharadron Overlords player can use this command ability in the combat phase if the general of the survivors contingent is on the battlefield. If they do so, until the end of that phase, when a friendly Kharadron Overlords model from the survivors contingent is slain within 12" of the general of the survivors contingent, roll a dice before the slain model is removed from play. On a 5+, that model can shoot before it is removed.

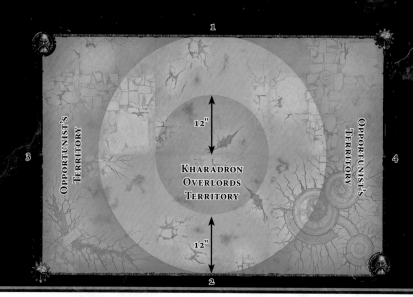

1

OPPORTUNIST'S TERRITORY

3

12"

KHARADRON OVERLORDS TERRITORY

12"

OPPORTUNIST'S TERRITORY

4

2

Here Comes the Fleet: *The commander of the relief force boldly promises the rescue of the beleaguered duardin on the ground.*

The Kharadron Overlords player can use this command ability in the battleshock phase if the general of the rescuers contingent is on the battlefield. If they do so, until the end of that phase, do not take battleshock tests for friendly **Kharadron Overlords** units wholly within 24" of the general of the rescuers contingent.

Strike Fast: *The general of the Kharadron's foes urges their warriors on, demanding that they kill the survivors of the crash before any reinforcements arrive.*

The Opportunist can use this command ability in their hero phase if their general is on the battlefield. If they do so, the Opportunist can re-roll run or charge rolls for Opportunist units until their next hero phase.

RIDE OF THE OVERLORDS

At the end of the Kharadron Overlords' first movement phase, the Kharadron Overlords player must set up the rescuers contingent. The Kharadron Overlords players rolls a dice and consults the map to see which edge of the battlefield corresponds with that roll. If the roll is a 5 or 6, they can choose the edge. They must set up all of the units in the rescuers contingents, wholly within 12" of that edge and more than 9" from any enemy units.

BATTLE LENGTH

The battle lasts until a player wins a **major victory** or for 5 battle rounds, whichever happens first.

GLORIOUS VICTORY

If the Opportunist has no models on the battlefield at the end of a battle round, the Kharadron Overlords player wins a **major victory**.

If the Kharadron Overlords player has no models from the survivors contingent on the battlefield at the end of a battle round, the Opportunist wins a **major victory**.

If half or more of the models from the survivors contingent are still on the battlefield at the end of the fifth battle round, the Kharadron Overlords player wins a **minor victory**.

If less than half of the models from the survivors contingent are still on the battlefield at the end of the fifth battle round, the Opportunist wins a **minor victory**.

PATH TO GLORY

Path to Glory campaigns centre around collecting and fighting a series of battles in the Mortal Realms. Players start off with a small warband. Over the course of several battles, each warband will gather more followers to join them in their quest for glory and renown.

In order to take part in a Path to Glory campaign, you will need two or more players. Each player will need a **Hero** to be their champion and must then create a warband to follow and fight beside their champion during the campaign.

The players fight battles against each other using the warbands they have created. The results of these battles will gain their warbands glory. After battle, warbands may swell in numbers as more warriors flock to their banner, or existing troops may become more powerful.

After gaining sufficient glory or growing your warband enough to dominate all others through sheer weight of numbers, you will be granted a final test. Succeed, and you will be crowned the victor of the campaign, your glory affirmed for all time.

CREATING A WARBAND
In a Path to Glory game, you do not select your army in the normal manner. Instead, you create a warband that consists of a mighty champion, battling to earn the favour of the gods, and their followers. The details and progress of each warband need to be recorded on a warband roster, which you can download for free from games-workshop.com.

To create a warband, simply follow these steps and record the results on your warband roster:

1. First, pick a faction for your warband. Each faction has its own set of warband tables that are used to generate the units in the warband and the rewards they can receive for fighting battles. The warband tables included in this battletome let you collect a Kharadron Overlords warband, but other Warhammer Age of Sigmar publications include warband tables to let you collect warbands from other factions.

2. Next, choose your warband's champion by selecting one of the options from your faction's champion table. Give your champion a suitably grand name and write this down on your warband roster.

3. Having picked your champion, the next step is to make follower rolls to generate your starting followers. The champion you chose in step 2 will determine how many follower rolls you have. To make a follower roll, pick a column from one of the followers tables and then roll a dice. If you prefer, instead of rolling a dice, you can pick the result from the followers table (this still uses up the roll).

Sometimes a table will require you to expend two or more rolls, or one roll and a number of Glory Points (see Gaining Glory), in order to use it. Note that the option to expend Glory Points can only be used when you add new followers to your warband after a battle (see Rewards of Battle). In either case, in order to generate a follower unit from the table, you must have enough rolls and/or Glory Points to meet the requirements, and you can then either roll once on the table or pick one result from the table of your choice. If you expend Glory Points, you must reduce your Glory Points total by the amount shown on the table.

Followers are organised into units. The followers table tells you how many models the unit has. Follower units cannot include additional models, but they can otherwise take any options listed on their warscroll. Record all of the information about your followers on your warband roster.

4. You can use 1 follower roll to allow your champion to start the campaign with a Champion's Reward or to allow 1 of your follower units to start the campaign with a Follower's Reward (see Rewards of Battle).

5. Finally, give your warband a name, one that will inspire respect and dread in your rivals. Your warband is now complete and you can fight your first battle. Good luck!

TO WAR!
Having created a warband, you can now fight battles with it against other warbands taking part in the campaign. You can fight battles as and when you wish, and you can use any of the battleplans available for Warhammer Age of Sigmar. The units you use for a game must be those on your roster.

When you use a Kharadron Overlords warband in a Path to Glory game, you can use all the battle traits from page 61 except the Sky-ports battle trait. You cannot use any other Kharadron Overlords allegiance abilities.

Any casualties suffered by a warband are assumed to have been replaced in time for its next battle. If your champion is slain in a battle, it is assumed that they were merely injured; they are back to full strength for your next game, thirsty for vengeance!

GAINING GLORY
All of the players in the campaign are vying for glory. The amount of glory they have received is represented by the Glory Points that the warband has accumulated.

As a warband's glory increases, it will also attract additional followers, and a warband's champion may be granted rewards.

Warbands receive Glory Points after a battle is complete. If the warband drew or lost the battle, it receives 1 Glory Point. If it won the battle, it receives D3 Glory Points (re-roll a result of 1 if it won a **major victory**).

Add the Glory Points you scored to the total recorded on your roster. Once you have won 10 Glory Points, you will have a chance to win the campaign (see Eternal Glory).

REWARDS OF BATTLE

After each battle, you can take one of the three following options. Alternatively, roll a D3 to determine which option to take.

D3   **Option**

1   **Additional Followers:** *More loyal followers flock to your banner.*

You receive 1 follower roll that can be used to select a new unit from a followers table and add it to your warband roster. See step 3 of Creating a Warband for details of how to use the followers table to add a unit to your warband. Once 5 new units have joined your warband, you will have a chance to win the campaign (see Eternal Glory).

2   **Champion's Reward:** *Your champion's prowess grows.*

Roll on your champion rewards table for your warband and note the result on your warband roster. Your champion can only receive one Champion's Reward – if they already have a Champion's Reward, you must take a Follower's Reward instead.

3   **Follower's Reward:** *Your warriors become renowned for mighty deeds.*

Pick 1 unit of followers and then roll on the followers rewards table for your warband. Note the result on your warband roster. A unit can only receive one Follower's Reward. If all of your follower units have a Follower's Reward, you must take Additional Followers instead.

ETERNAL GLORY

There are two ways to win a Path to Glory campaign: by Blood or by Might. To win by Blood, your warband must first have 10 Glory Points. To win by Might, your warband must have at least 5 additional units of followers. In either case, you must then fight and win one more battle to win the campaign. If the next battle you fight is tied or lost, you do not receive any Glory Points – just keep on fighting battles until you win the campaign… or another player wins first!

You can shorten or lengthen a campaign by lowering or raising the number of Glory Points needed to win by Blood or the number of extra units that must join a warband to win by Might. For example, for a shorter campaign, you could say that a warband only needs 5 Glory Points before the final fight, or for a longer one, you could say that 15 are needed.

KHARADRON OVERLORDS WARBAND TABLES

Use the following tables to determine the champion that leads your warband, the followers that make up the other units in the warband, and the rewards the warband receives after battle.

CHAMPION TABLE

Champion	Follower Rolls
Arkanaut Admiral	4
Endrinmaster with Dirigible Suit	2

HERO FOLLOWERS TABLE
(uses 1 roll)

D6	Followers
1-2	Endrinmaster with Endrinharness
3-4	Aetheric Navigator
5-6	Aether-Khemist

SKYFARERS FOLLOWERS TABLE
(uses 1 roll)

D6	Followers
1-2	10 Arkanaut Company
3-4	5 Grundstok Thunderers
5-6	3 Skywardens or Endrinriggers

SKYVESSEL FOLLOWERS TABLE
(uses number of rolls and glory points shown below)

D6	Followers
1-3	Grundstok Gunhauler (2 rolls, or 1 roll and 1 glory point)
4-5	Arkanaut Frigate (3 rolls, or 1 roll and 2 glory points)
6	Arkanaut Ironclad (5 rolls, or 1 roll and 4 glory points)

SKYFARERS REWARDS TABLE

D6 Reward

1 Deeds, Not Words: *These warriors see great honour in taking the fight straight to the foe.*

Add 1 to wound rolls for attacks made with melee weapons by this unit if it made a charge move in the same turn.

2 Incredibly Stubborn: *These duardin are extremely tenacious, and will often deny death long enough to get in one last telling blow.*

If a model from this unit is slain while it is within 3" of enemy unit, roll a dice. On a 6, that model can fight before it is removed from play.

3 Fearsome Raiders: *These skyfarers attack rapidly from unexpected quarters, striking fear into the hearts of their foes.*

Subtract 1 from the Bravery characteristic of enemy units while they are within 6" of any friendly units with this ability.

4 Bold Privateers: *These duardin are trained to swiftly disembark from their skyvessel and then charge headlong into the foe.*

This unit can leave a friendly **ARKANAUT FRIGATE** either before or after it has moved. Roll 3D6 instead of 2D6 when making charge rolls for this unit if it left a friendly **ARKANAUT FRIGATE** in the movement phase of the same turn.

5 Focused Fire: *These skyfarers are adept at concentrating their fire upon a single target, destroying it with one devastating volley.*

At the start of your shooting phase, you can pick 1 enemy unit for this unit to focus fire on. If you do so, models from this unit can only target that unit in that phase, but you can re-roll hit rolls of 1 for attacks made by this unit in that phase.

6 Carefully Trained: You can pick the result you wish to apply to the unit.

CHAMPION AND HERO REWARDS TABLE

D6 Reward

1 Opportunistic Privateer: *This feared buccaneer strikes swiftly and without warning, crushing their enemies before they have a chance to react.*

If this model is on the battlefield after armies are set up but before the first battle round begins, you can pick this model and up to 2 other friendly units. Remove this model and those units from the battlefield and then set them up again anywhere on the battlefield more than 9" from any enemy units and so that all of the units are wholly within 12" of this model. Units set up in this way cannot make a normal move in the first battle round.

2 Champion of Progress: *This champion is at the very forefront of the Kharadron Overlords' advance, and their confidence is palpable.*

Do not take battleshock for friendly units while they are wholly within 12" of this model.

3 Valorous: *This champion has become renowned for their exceptional valour.*

The first time this model is slain, before removing them, roll a dice. On a 2+ they are not slain, you can heal up to D3 wounds allocated to them, and any wounds remaining to be allocated to them are negated.

4-5 Command Trait: *This champion has become a master of their craft.*

Randomly generate 1 command trait for this champion from one of the command trait tables on pages 62-63.

6 Artefact of Power: *An ancient artefact of power has come into this champion's possession.*

Randomly generate 1 artefact of power for this champion from one of the artefact of power tables on pages 62-63.

SKYVESSEL REWARDS TABLE

D6 Reward

1 Master Helmsmen: *The skyfarer that controls this vessel's wheel is exceptionally skilled.*

You can re-roll run and charge rolls for this model.

2 Master Gunner: *The skyfarer that commands this vessel's guns is a hard taskmaster.*

You can re-roll 1 hit roll for this model each phase.

3 Windrider: *This vessel catches the aetheric winds like no other.*

Add 1" to this model's Move characteristic.

4 Focused Fire: *The crew of this skyvessel are trained to concentrate their fire upon a single target, destroying it with one devastating volley.*

At the start of your shooting phase, you can pick 1 enemy unit for this model to focus fire on. If you do so, this model can only target that unit in that phase, but you can re-roll hit rolls of 1 for attacks made by this model in that phase.

5-6 Great Endrinworks: *This skyvessel has been upgraded with an endrinwork produced by a master shipwright.*

Randomly generate 1 great endrinwork for this model from one of the great endrinworks tables on pages 66-67.

WARSCROLLS

This section includes the Kharadron Overlords warscrolls and warscroll battalions. Updated January 2020; the warscrolls printed here take precedence over any warscrolls with an earlier publication date or no publication date.

WARSCROLL BATTALION
GRAND ARMADA

When the stakes are high, an Arkanaut Admiral will take personal command of a Grand Armada, gathering a mighty assemblage of skyvessels bristling with aethermatic weaponry and Kharadron privateers who won't let anything get between them and their share of the impressive haul promised them by their Captains.

ORGANISATION

- 1 Arkanaut Admiral or Brokk Grungsson

- 1 Iron Sky Command

- 1 Iron Sky Attack Squadron

- 1-3 Grundstok Escort Wings

ABILITIES

Constitutional Experts: *The leader of a Grand Armada is able to wring the maximum advantage from the Kharadron Code.*

Once per battle, if the **Arkanaut Admiral** or **Brokk Grungsson** from this battalion is on the battlefield, you can use a footnote even if it has been used before in the same battle.

WARSCROLL BATTALION
IRON SKY COMMAND

ORGANISATION

- 0-1 Arkanaut Admiral or Brokk Grungsson

- 1 Arkanaut Ironclad

- 3 units chosen from the following list in any combination: Aether-Khemist, Aetheric Navigator, **ENDRINMASTER**

- 1 Arkanaut Company unit

- 1-3 Endrinriggers units

ABILITIES

Lords of the Skies: *Kharadron are filled with confidence while the flagship of the Iron Sky Command is nearby.*

Do not take battleshock tests for friendly **KHARADRON OVERLORDS** units while they are wholly within 18" of the **ARKANAUT IRONCLAD** from this battalion.

WARSCROLL BATTALION
IRON SKY ATTACK SQUADRON

ORGANISATION

- 2+ Arkanaut Frigates

- 1 Arkanaut Company unit for each Arkanaut Frigate in the same battalion

ABILITIES

Bold Privateers: *The Arkanaut Companies in an Iron Sky Squadron are trained to swiftly disembark from their skyvessels and then charge headlong into the foe.*

ARKANAUT COMPANY units from this battalion can leave an **ARKANAUT FRIGATE** from the same battalion either before or after it has moved. In addition, roll 3D6 instead of 2D6 when making charge rolls for **ARKANAUT COMPANY** units from this battalion that left an **ARKANAUT FRIGATE** from the same battalion in the movement phase of the same turn.

WARSCROLL BATTALION
GRUNDSTOK ESCORT WING

ORGANISATION

- 2-3 Grundstok Gunhaulers

- 1 Arkanaut Ironclad or Arkanaut Frigate

- 1 Grundstok Thunderers unit

- 0-3 Skywardens units

ABILITIES

Focused Fire: *The units that make up a Grundstok Escort Wing are trained to concentrate their fire upon a single target, destroying it in one devastating volley.*

At the start of your shooting phase, you can pick 1 enemy unit for this battalion to focus fire on. If you do so, you can re-roll hit rolls of 1 for attacks made by units from this battalion that target that unit in that phase.

BROKK GRUNGSSON
LORD-MAGNATE OF BARAK-NAR

MOVE	12"
WOUNDS	8
SAVE	3+
BRAVERY	8

82

Lord-Magnate Brokk Grungsson is the richest Kharadron privateer alive. Clad in a custom-built endrinharness and carrying a small armoury of lethal firearms, he seeks out fresh sources of aether-gold with single-minded belligerence.

MISSILE WEAPONS	Range	Attacks	To Hit	To Wound	Rend	Damage
Grungsson's Boast	18"	2	3+	2+	-2	D3
The Magnate's Charter	18"	6	3+	3+	-1	1
Aetherblasters	9"	2	3+	4+	-	1
MELEE WEAPONS	Range	Attacks	To Hit	To Wound	Rend	Damage
Aethermatic Saw	1"	4	3+	2+	-2	D3

DESCRIPTION

Brokk Grungsson is a named character that is a single model. He is armed with Grungsson's Boast, the Magnate's Charter, Aetherblasters and an Aethermatic Saw.

FLY: This model can fly.

ABILITIES

Custom-built Dirigible Suit: *When Brokk Grungsson charges into combat his foes are crushed by the weight of his magnificent custom-built dirigible suit.*

After this model makes a charge move, you can pick 1 enemy unit within 1" of this model and roll a dice. On a 2+, that enemy unit suffers D3 mortal wounds.

Endrinharness: *An Endrinharness is supercharged with energy, allowing the wearer to strike mighty blows in close combat.*

If the unmodified hit roll for an attack made with a melee weapon by this model is 6, that attack inflicts D3 mortal wounds and the attack sequence ends (do not make a wound or save roll).

Hitcher: *Kharadron kitted out with buoyancy endrins can attach themselves to a passing skyvessel and move alongside it.*

If this model is wholly within 6" of a friendly **Skyvessel** immediately before the **Skyvessel** uses its Fly High ability, you can say that this model will hitch a lift instead of making a normal move (as long as this model has not already made a normal move in the same phase).

If you do so, after that **Skyvessel** has moved, remove this model from the battlefield and set it up again wholly within 6" of that **Skyvessel**, more than 1" from any terrain features or objectives and more than 9" from any enemy models.

No more than 7 models can hitch a lift on the same **Skyvessel** in the same turn.

COMMAND ABILITIES

First Rule of Grungsson: *When Brokk Grungsson leads his warriors into battle, he reminds them of his first and most significant commentary on the Code – 'to the victor, the spoils'.*

You can use this command ability at the start of your charge phase if a friendly model with this command ability is on the battlefield. If you do so, pick 1 friendly model with this command ability. You can re-roll charge rolls for friendly **Barak-Nar** units that are wholly within 24" of that model until the end of that phase.

KEYWORDS	ORDER, DUARDIN, KHARADRON OVERLORDS, BARAK-NAR, HERO, SKYFARER, BROKK GRUNGSSON

Lord-Magnate Brokk Grungsson's practically limitless personal wealth allows him to employ the very finest soldiers of Barak-Nar in his endless pursuit of riches, along with massive Ironclads fresh from the shipwrights' yard.

ENDRINMASTER
WITH DIRIGIBLE SUIT

	MOVE 12"	
WOUNDS 8		SAVE 3+
	8	
	BRAVERY	

84

Many Endrinmasters take to the skies in mastercrafted dirigible suits, their aetherturbines allowing them to zoom through the air towards skyvessels in need of repair even as an in-built weapon array blasts their enemies into pieces.

MISSILE WEAPONS	Range	Attacks	To Hit	To Wound	Rend	Damage
Aethercannon	12"	1	3+	2+	-2	D3
Dirigible Suit Weapon Battery	18"	6	3+	3+	-1	1
Gaze of Grungni	9"	1	3+	2+	-1	D3
MELEE WEAPONS	Range	Attacks	To Hit	To Wound	Rend	Damage
Aethermatic Saw	1"	3	3+	2+	-2	D3

DESCRIPTION

An Endrinmaster with Dirigible Suit is a single model armed with an Aethercannon, Dirigible Suit Weapon Battery, Gaze of Grungni and Aethermatic Saw.

FLY: This model can fly.

ABILITIES

Endrinmaster: *Endrinmasters are unsurpassed at keeping the skyvessels in a fleet battleworthy.*

At the start of your hero phase, you can pick 1 friendly **SKYVESSEL** within 1" of this model. Heal 3 wounds allocated to that **SKYVESSEL**.

Hitcher: *Kharadron kitted out with buoyancy endrins can attach themselves to a passing skyvessel and move alongside it.*

If this model is wholly within 6" of a friendly **SKYVESSEL** immediately before the **SKYVESSEL** uses its Fly High ability, you can say that this model will hitch a lift instead of making a normal move (as long as this model has not already made a normal move in the same phase).

If you do so, after that **SKYVESSEL** has moved, remove this model from the battlefield and set it up again wholly within 6" of that **SKYVESSEL**, more than 1" from any terrain features or objectives and more than 9" from any enemy models.

No more than 7 models can hitch a lift on the same **SKYVESSEL** in the same turn.

COMMAND ABILITIES

By Grungni, I Have My Eye On You!:
Endrinriggers will redouble their efforts to repair a skyvessel when they are overseen by an Endrinmaster.

You can use this command ability in your hero phase before a friendly **ENDRINRIGGERS** unit wholly within 18" of a friendly model with this command ability uses its Endrincraft ability.

If you do so, you can re-roll any of the dice that determine how many wounds are healed by that **ENDRINRIGGERS** unit in that phase.

KEYWORDS	ORDER, DUARDIN, KHARADRON OVERLORDS, HERO, SKYFARER, ENDRINMASTER

ARKANAUT ADMIRAL

85

	MOVE
WOUNDS 6	4"
8	SAVE 3+
	BRAVERY

Arkanaut Admirals are the cream of the sky-ports' officer class, intrepid leaders and battle-hardened veterans of a thousand aerial engagements whose booming commands inspire their crew to mighty deeds in the search for profit.

MISSILE WEAPONS	Range	Attacks	To Hit	To Wound	Rend	Damage
Volley Pistol	9"	3	3+	4+	-1	1
MELEE WEAPONS	Range	Attacks	To Hit	To Wound	Rend	Damage
Skalfhammer	1"	3	3+	2+	-2	2

DESCRIPTION

An Arkanaut Admiral is a single model armed with a Skalfhammer and a Volley Pistol.

ABILITIES

If You Want A Job Done…: *Every Arkanaut Admiral knows that there are some foes that you have to deal with yourself.*

You can re-roll hit and wound rolls of 1 for attacks made with a melee weapon by this model that target a **Hero** or **Monster**.

Protect the Admiral!: *The skyfarers that follow an Admiral will lay down their own lives to protect them.*

Do not take battleshock tests for friendly **Kharadron Overlords** units while they are wholly within 12" of this model.

In addition, roll a dice before you allocate a wound or mortal wound to a friendly **Arkanaut Admiral** while it is within 3" of any friendly **Skyfarers** units with 5 or more models. On a 5+, you must allocate that wound or mortal wound to a friendly **Skyfarers** unit with 5 or more models that is within 3" of that **Arkanaut Admiral**, instead of to that **Arkanaut Admiral**.

COMMAND ABILITIES

Master of the Skies: *The Admiral knows how to get every last bit of speed from the skyvessels they command.*

You can use this command ability at the start of your shooting phase. If you do so, pick 1 friendly **Skyvessel** that has a model with this command ability in its garrison. That **Skyvessel** can shoot in that phase even if it ran earlier in the same turn.

On My Mark, Fire!: *An Admiral times the fire of their skyvessel so as to inflict the maximum possible amount of damage on the foe.*

You can use this command ability at the start of your shooting phase. If you do so, pick 1 friendly **Skyvessel** that has a model with this command ability in its garrison. You can re-roll hit rolls of 1 for attacks made by that **Skyvessel** in that phase.

Repel Boarders!: *The Admiral directs his crew to drive off anybody that dares to board his precious skyvessel.*

You can use this command ability at the start of your combat phase. If you do so, pick 1 friendly **Skyvessel** that has a model with this command ability in its garrison. Add 1 to hit rolls for attacks made by that **Skyvessel** and any models in its garrison in that phase.

Up And At Them!: *The Admiral leaps ashore, and orders any Kharadron that are nearby to charge the foe.*

You can use this command ability at the start of your charge phase. If you do so, pick 1 friendly **Skyfarers** unit that is wholly within 12" of a friendly model with this command ability. You can re-roll charge rolls for that unit in that phase.

KEYWORDS	ORDER, DUARDIN, KHARADRON OVERLORDS, HERO, SKYFARER, MARINE, ARKANAUT ADMIRAL

MOVE		4"	
WOUNDS	5	✕	SAVE 3+
		7	
	BRAVERY		

86

AETHERIC NAVIGATOR

Utilising cutting-edge aethermatic science in order to decipher the ever-changing wind patterns of the Mortal Realms, Aetheric Navigators are an invaluable presence upon any Kharadron skyvessel.

MISSILE WEAPONS	Range	Attacks	To Hit	To Wound	Rend	Damage
Ranging Pistol	15"	2	3+	3+	-1	1
MELEE WEAPONS	Range	Attacks	To Hit	To Wound	Rend	Damage
Zephyrscope	1"	2	3+	4+	-	1

DESCRIPTION

An Aetheric Navigator is a single model armed with a Zephyrscope and a Ranging Pistol.

ABILITIES

Aethersight: *Aetheric Navigators can unpick enemy spells by harnessing the arcane jet streams.*

This model can attempt to dispel 1 endless spell at the start of your hero phase and attempt to unbind 1 spell in the enemy hero phase, in the same manner as a WIZARD.

Aetherstorm: *An Aetheric Navigator can manipulate the aether to cause a localised storm.*

In your hero phase, you can pick 1 enemy unit within 36" of this model that is visible to them and can fly, and roll a dice. On a 1-2 nothing happens. On a 3-5 halve the Move characteristic of that unit until your next hero phase. On a 6, halve the Move characteristic of that unit until your next hero phase, and that unit suffers D3 mortal wounds.

Read the Winds: *Navigators can signal to nearby Kharadron Overlords airships, helping them to steer into prevailing currents.*

You can re-roll run and charge rolls for friendly SKYVESSELS that are visible to a friendly AETHERIC NAVIGATOR that has not attempted to use the Aetherstorm ability in the same turn.

KEYWORDS	ORDER, DUARDIN, KHARADRON OVERLORDS, HERO, SKYFARER, MARINE, AETHERIC NAVIGATOR

Though they are most at home aboard the deck of a Kharadron battleship, Aetheric Navigators can employ their aether-instruments to aid their allies, either by suffocating enemy magic with a gust of magical wind, or simply by blasting their foes with a heavy ranging pistol.

ENDRINMASTER
WITH ENDRINHARNESS

Endrinmasters are peerless combat mechanics, well used to conducting emergency repairs in the white heat of battle. Many equip themselves with a strength-enhancing endrinharness that allows them to wield a fearsome aethermight hammer.

MISSILE WEAPONS	Range	Attacks	To Hit	To Wound	Rend	Damage
Gaze of Grungni	9"	1	3+	2+	-1	D3
MELEE WEAPONS	Range	Attacks	To Hit	To Wound	Rend	Damage
Aethermight Hammer	1"	3	3+	3+	-1	D3

DESCRIPTION
An Endrinmaster with Endrinharness is a single model armed with an Aethermight Hammer and Gaze of Grungni.

ABILITIES
Endrinmaster: *Endrinmasters are unsurpassed at keeping the skyvessels in a fleet battleworthy.*

At the start of your hero phase, you can pick 1 friendly **SKYVESSEL** within 1" of this model. Heal up to D3 wounds allocated to that **SKYVESSEL**.

Endrinharness: *An Endrinharness is supercharged with energy, allowing the wearer to strike mighty blows in close combat.*

If the unmodified hit roll for an attack made with a melee weapon by this model is 6, that attack inflicts 3 mortal wounds and the attack sequence ends (do not make a wound or save roll).

COMMAND ABILITIES
By Grungni, I Have My Eye On You!:
Endrinriggers will redouble their efforts to repair a skyvessel when they are overseen by an Endrinmaster.

You can use this command ability in your hero phase before a friendly **ENDRINRIGGER** unit wholly within 18" of a friendly model with this command ability uses its Endrincraft ability. If you do so, you can re-roll any of the dice that determine how many wounds are healed by that **ENDRINRIGGER** unit in that phase.

KEYWORDS | ORDER, DUARDIN, KHARADRON OVERLORDS, HERO, SKYFARER, MARINE, ENDRINMASTER

AETHER-KHEMIST

Masters of alchemy and atmospheric analysis, Aether-Khemists not only augment their comrades' weapons with a boost of aether-gold, but can also turn their esoteric devices against their foes to drain the air from their lungs.

MISSILE WEAPONS	Range	Attacks	To Hit	To Wound	Rend	Damage
Atmospheric Anatomiser	9"	3D6	4+	4+	-2	1
MELEE WEAPONS	Range	Attacks	To Hit	To Wound	Rend	Damage
Heavy Instruments	1"	2	4+	4+	-	1

DESCRIPTION
An Aether-Khemist is a single model armed with an Atmospheric Anatomiser and Heavy Instruments.

ABILITIES
Aetheric Augmentation: *An Aether-Khemist can use their Atmospheric Anatomiser to augment the weapons of nearby skyfarers.*

In your hero phase you can pick 1 friendly **SKYFARERS** unit wholly within 12" of this model. Until your next hero phase, you can re-roll wound rolls of 1 for attacks made by that unit. This ability cannot be used by an **AETHER-KHEMIST** that is part of a garrison, or on a friendly unit that is part of a garrison.

Atmospheric Isolation: *An Aether-Khemist can use their Anatomiser to create a vacuum around themselves, suffocating their foes.*

Subtract 1 from hit rolls for attacks made by enemy models while they are within 3" of any friendly models with this ability. This ability cannot be used by an **AETHER-KHEMIST** that is part of a garrison.

KEYWORDS | ORDER, DUARDIN, KHARADRON OVERLORDS, HERO, SKYFARER, MARINE, AETHER-KHEMIST

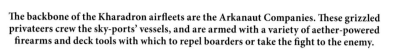

ARKANAUT COMPANY

88

MOVE **4"**

WOUNDS **1**

SAVE **4+**

BRAVERY **6**

The backbone of the Kharadron airfleets are the Arkanaut Companies. These grizzled privateers crew the sky-ports' vessels, and are armed with a variety of aether-powered firearms and deck tools with which to repel boarders or take the fight to the enemy.

MISSILE WEAPONS	Range	Attacks	To Hit	To Wound	Rend	Damage
Privateer Pistol	9"	2	4+	4+	-	1
Aethermatic Volley Gun	12"	6	5+	4+	-1	1
Light Skyhook	18"	1	4+	3+	-2	D3
Aetherflare Pistol	9"	2	4+	3+	-	1
Volley Pistol	9"	3	4+	4+	-	1
MELEE WEAPONS	Range	Attacks	To Hit	To Wound	Rend	Damage
Arkanaut Cutter	1"	1	4+	4+	-	1
Gun Butt	1"	1	4+	5+	-	1
Skypike	2"	2	4+	4+	-1	D3

DESCRIPTION

An Arkanaut Company has any number of models, each armed with a Privateer Pistol and Arkanaut Cutter.

1 in every 10 models can replace their Privateer Pistol and Arkanaut Cutter with an Aethermatic Volley Gun and Gun Butt; 1 in every 10 models can replace their Privateer Pistol and Arkanaut Cutter with a Light Skyhook and Gun Butt; and 1 in every 10 models can replace their Privateer Pistol and Arkanaut Cutter with a Skypike.

COMPANY CAPTAIN: 1 model in this unit can be a Company Captain. That model is armed with an Aetherflare Pistol or Volley Pistol instead of a Privateer Pistol.

ABILITIES

Glory-seekers: *All of the warriors that make up an Arkanaut Company are eager to win recognition for daring deeds.*

You can re-roll battleshock tests for this unit while it is wholly within 9" of an objective, and add 1 to hit rolls for attacks made by this unit while it is wholly within 9" of an objective. This ability cannot be used if this unit is part of a garrison.

KEYWORDS ORDER, DUARDIN, KHARADRON OVERLORDS, SKYFARER, MARINE, ARKANAUT COMPANY

BJORGEN THUNDRIK

MOVE	4"
WOUNDS	5
SAVE	4+
BRAVERY	7

89

The dauntless leader of a band of profiteers, Bjorgen Thundrik has developed quite the reputation in Barak-Nar for being able to sniff out fresh seams of aethergold, and for being utterly tenacious in his pursuit of riches.

MISSILE WEAPONS	Range	Attacks	To Hit	To Wound	Rend	Damage
Atmospheric Anatomiser	9"	3D6	4+	4+	-2	1
MELEE WEAPONS	Range	Attacks	To Hit	To Wound	Rend	Damage
Heavy Instruments	1"	3	4+	4+	-	1

DESCRIPTION

Bjorgen Thundrik is a named character that is a single model. He is armed with an Atmospheric Anatomiser and Heavy Instruments.

ABILITIES

Aetheric Augmentation: *An Aether-Khemist can use their Atmospheric Anatomiser to augment the weapons of nearby skyfarers.*

In your hero phase you can pick 1 friendly **SKYFARERS** unit wholly within 12" of this model and that is not part of a garrison. Until your next hero phase, you can re-roll hit rolls of 1 for that unit. This ability cannot be used by a model that is part of a garrison.

Atmospheric Isolation: *An Aether-Khemist can use their Anatomiser to create a vacuum around themselves, suffocating their foes.*

Subtract 1 from hit rolls for attacks made by enemy models while they are within 3" of any friendly models with this ability. This ability cannot be used by a model that is part of a garrison.

KEYWORDS	ORDER, DUARDIN, KHARADRON OVERLORDS, BARAK-NAR, HERO, SKYFARER, MARINE, AETHER-KHEMIST, BJORGEN THUNDRIK

THUNDRIK'S PROFITEERS

MOVE	4"
WOUNDS	1
SAVE	4+
BRAVERY	7

Driven by constant competition for promotion, this eclectic band of skyfarers will go to any lengths to secure a valuable haul, and will pepper with volleys of aethershot all those who try to take their wealth.

MISSILE WEAPONS	Range	Attacks	To Hit	To Wound	Rend	Damage
Aethermatic Volley Gun	18"	6	5+	4+	-1	1
Aethershot Rifle	18"	4	3+	4+	-1	1
Privateer Pistol	12"	2	4+	4+	-	1
Vulcaniser Pistol	9"	2	3+	3+	-1	1
MELEE WEAPONS	Range	Attacks	To Hit	To Wound	Rend	Damage
Arkanaut Cutter	1"	2	4+	4+	-	1
Gun Butt	1"	1	4+	4+	-	1
Skypike	2"	2	4+	3+	-1	D3

DESCRIPTION

Thundrik's Profiteers is a unit that has 4 models. Garodd Alensen is armed with a Privateer Pistol and Arkanaut Cutter; Enrik Ironhail is armed with an Aethermatic Volley Gun and Gun Butt; Dead-Eye Lund is armed with an Aethershot Rifle and Gun Butt; and Khazgan Drakkskewer is armed with a Vulcaniser Pistol and Skypike.

KHAZGAN DRAKKSKEWER: Add 1 to Khazgan Drakkskewer's Wounds characteristic. In addition, Khazgan Drakkskewer can fly.

ABILITIES

Thundrik's Profiteers: *The Profiteers are ever eager to win Thundrik's recognition.*

You can add 1 to hit rolls for attacks made by this unit and re-roll battleshock tests for this unit while it is wholly within 9" of **BJORGEN THUNDRIK**. This ability cannot be used if this unit is part of a garrison.

KEYWORDS	ORDER, DUARDIN, KHARADRON OVERLORDS, BARAK-NAR, SKYFARER, MARINE, THUNDRIK'S PROFITEERS

90

MOVE ✴

18 ✕ **3+** SAVE

8

BRAVERY

WOUNDS

ARKANAUT IRONCLAD

Amongst the heaviest Kharadron ships of the line, the redoubtable Ironclads provide a floating fortress of iron at the heart of any airfleet, bombarding their targets from afar with explosives shells and armour-piercing torpedoes.

MISSILE WEAPONS	Range	Attacks	To Hit	To Wound	Rend	Damage
Great Sky Cannon: Shrapnel	24"	6	3+	3+	-1	2
Great Sky Cannon: Shell	30"	1	3+	2+	-2	6
Great Skyhook	24"	1	3+	2+	-2	6
Great Volley Cannon	18"	4D6	3+	3+	-1	1
Aethershock Torpedoes	24"	4	4+	3+	-1	D3
Aethershot Carbines	12"	8	3+	3+	-1	2
MELEE WEAPONS	**Range**	**Attacks**	**To Hit**	**To Wound**	**Rend**	**Damage**
Boarding Weapons	1"	✴	4+	4+	-	1

DAMAGE TABLE			
Wounds Suffered	Move	Boarding Weapons	Bomb Racks
0-3	10", Disengage, Fly High	8	+2
4-6	8", Disengage, Fly High	7	+1
7-9	6", Disengage	6	0
10-15	6"	5	0
16+	4"	4	-1

DESCRIPTION

An Arkanaut Ironclad is a single model armed with Aethershot Carbines, Aethershock Torpedoes, Boarding Weapons and one of the following weapon options: Great Sky Cannon; Great Skyhook; or Great Volley Cannon.

FLYING TRANSPORT: This model can fly, and can be garrisoned by up to 25 friendly **MARINE** models even though it is not a terrain feature.

Halve this model's Move characteristic and it cannot Fly High if there are 16 or more models in its garrison. Units cannot join or leave this model's garrison if it has made a move or flown high in the same phase (they can join or leave before it does so). Models in the garrison are not counted towards gaining control of an objective.

An attack made by a weapon that is in range of this model can target either this model or a unit in its garrison. If this model is destroyed, before it is removed from play, roll 1 dice for each model in its garrison. On a 1, that model is slain. Set up any surviving models wholly within 3" of this model and more than 3" from any enemy units.

ABILITIES

Aetheric Navigator and Endrinrigger: *A skyvessel's Navigator guides it into the strongest aetheric winds, while its Endrinrigger works tirelessly to keep it airworthy.*

In your hero phase, you can heal 1 wound allocated to this model. In addition, you can re-roll run rolls for this model.

Bomb Racks: *The bombs and skymines held in the racks of a Kharadron skyvessel can be swiftly deployed to stop enemy assaults in their tracks.*

At the start of the combat phase, you can pick 1 enemy unit within 1" of this model and roll a dice. Add the Bomb Rack modifier from this model's damage table to the roll. On a 4+, that enemy unit suffers D3 mortal wounds.

Disengage: *Kharadron skyvessels can easily disengage from ground-based foes, flying away with all guns blazing.*

This model and any models in its garrison can still shoot if this model retreats in the same turn, as long as there are no enemy units that can fly within 3" of this model at the start of the retreat move and there are less than 10 wounds allocated to this model at the start of the retreat move.

Fly High: *Kharadron skyvessels can swiftly soar up high in the air and then dive back down to the battlefield, ready to attack from a new direction.*

Instead of making a normal move with this model, if there are less than 7 wounds currently allocated to this model, you can say that it will fly high (it can retreat and disengage). If you do so, remove this model from the battlefield and set it up again more than 1" from any terrain features or objectives and more than 9" from any enemy models.

Great Skyhook: *Skyhooks are used to pull skyvessels towards the foe.*

Add 2 to charge rolls for this model if it is armed with a Great Skyhook.

Great Sky Cannon: *A sky cannon can either be loaded with shrapnel or an explosive shell.*

Before attacking with a Great Sky Cannon, choose either the Shrapnel or Shell missile weapon characteristics for that shooting attack.

KEYWORDS	ORDER, DUARDIN, KHARADRON OVERLORDS, WAR MACHINE, SKYVESSEL, ARKANAUT IRONCLAD

ARKANAUT FRIGATE

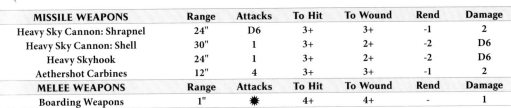

MOVE	14				
SAVE	4+				
WOUNDS	8				
BRAVERY					

The sleek and deadly profile of a Arkanaut Frigate is a sight greatly feared by the Kharadron's many enemies, who know all too well the devastating firepower these airships possess, and the fighting spirit of the privateers they carry into battle.

MISSILE WEAPONS	Range	Attacks	To Hit	To Wound	Rend	Damage
Heavy Sky Cannon: Shrapnel	24"	D6	3+	3+	-1	2
Heavy Sky Cannon: Shell	30"	1	3+	2+	-2	D6
Heavy Skyhook	24"	1	3+	2+	-2	D6
Aethershot Carbines	12"	4	3+	3+	-1	2
MELEE WEAPONS	Range	Attacks	To Hit	To Wound	Rend	Damage
Boarding Weapons	1"	✦	4+	4+	-	1

DAMAGE TABLE			
Wounds Suffered	Move	Boarding Weapons	Bomb Racks
0-3	12", Disengage, Fly High	6	+1
4-6	10", Disengage, Fly High	5	0
7-9	8", Disengage	4	0
10-12	6"	3	-1
13+	4"	2	-1

DESCRIPTION

An Arkanaut Frigate is a single model armed with Aethershot Carbines, Boarding Weapons and one of the following weapon options: Heavy Sky Cannon; or Heavy Skyhook.

FLYING TRANSPORT: This model can fly, and can be garrisoned by up to 15 friendly **MARINE** models even though it is not a terrain feature.

Halve this model's Move characteristic and it cannot Fly High if there are 11 or more models in its garrison. Units cannot join or leave this model's garrison if it has made a move or flown high in the same phase (they can join or leave before it does so). Models in the garrison are not counted towards gaining control of an objective.

An attack made by a weapon that is in range of this model can target either this model or a unit in its garrison. If this model is destroyed, before it is removed from play, roll 1 dice for each model in its garrison. On a 1, that model is slain. Set up any surviving models wholly within 3" of this model and more than 3" from any enemy units.

ABILITIES

Aetheric Navigator and Endrinrigger: *A skyvessel's Navigator guides it into the strongest aetheric winds, while its Endrinrigger works tirelessly to keep it airworthy.*

In your hero phase, you can heal 1 wound allocated to this model. In addition, you can re-roll run rolls for this model.

Bomb Racks: *The bombs and skymines held in the racks of a Kharadron skyvessel can be swiftly deployed to stop enemy assaults in their tracks.*

At the start of the combat phase, you can pick 1 enemy unit within 1" of this model and roll a dice. Add the Bomb Rack modifier from this model's damage table to the roll. On a 4+, that enemy unit suffers D3 mortal wounds.

Disengage: *Kharadron skyvessels can easily disengage from ground-based foes, flying away with all guns blazing.*

This model and any models in its garrison can still shoot if this model retreats in the same turn, as long as there are no enemy units that can fly within 3" of this model at the start of the retreat move and there are less than 10 wounds allocated to this model at the start of the retreat move.

Fly High: *Kharadron skyvessels can swiftly soar up high in the air and then dive back down to the battlefield, ready to attack from a new direction.*

Instead of making a normal move with this model, if there are less than 7 wounds currently allocated to this model, you can say that it will fly high (it can retreat and disengage). If you do so, remove this model from the battlefield and set it up again more than 1" from any terrain features or objectives and more than 9" from any enemy models.

Heavy Skyhook: *Skyhooks are used to pull skyvessels towards the foe.*

Add 2 to charge rolls for this model if it is armed with a Heavy Skyhook.

Heavy Sky Cannon: *A sky cannon can either be loaded with shrapnel or an explosive shell.*

Before attacking with a Heavy Sky Cannon, choose either the Shrapnel or Shell missile weapon characteristics for that shooting attack.

KEYWORDS	ORDER, DUARDIN, KHARADRON OVERLORDS, WAR MACHINE, SKYVESSEL, ARKANAUT FRIGATE

GRUNDSTOK GUNHAULER

MOVE	12"	
WOUNDS	10	SAVE 4+
	7	
BRAVERY		

92

Small, manoeuvrable and deadly, the Grundstok Gunhauler is an escort-class ship tasked with ensuring the safety of the airfleets' larger skyvessels. They perform this role well, swarming in defence before peeling off to launch deadly attack runs.

MISSILE WEAPONS	Range	Attacks	To Hit	To Wound	Rend	Damage
Sky Cannon: Shrapnel	18"	D6	3+	3+	-1	2
Sky Cannon: Shell	24"	1	3+	2+	-2	D6
Drill Cannon	36"	1	3+	3+	-3	D3
Aethershot Carbine	12"	2	3+	4+	-1	1
MELEE WEAPONS	Range	Attacks	To Hit	To Wound	Rend	Damage
Boarding Weapons	1"	4	4+	4+	-	1

DESCRIPTION
A Grundstok Gunhauler is a single model armed with an Aethershot Carbine, Boarding Weapons and one of the following weapon options: Sky Cannon; or Drill Cannon.

FLY: This model can fly.

ABILITIES
Ahead Full: *The Captain of a Grundstok Gunhauler can overcharge its engine so that the craft moves at maximum speed for a short time.*

Once per battle, at the start of your movement phase, you can say that this model will move ahead full. If you do so, add 6" to the Move characteristic of this model in that phase.

Escort Vessel: *Grundstok Gunhaulers are used to disrupt attacks on larger Kharadron skyvessels in the vicinity.*

Roll 1 dice each time you allocate a wound or mortal wound to a friendly **SKYVESSEL** other than a **GRUNDSTOK GUNHAULER** while it is within 3" of any friendly **GRUNDSTOK GUNHAULERS**. On a 6, that wound or mortal wound is negated.

Bomb Racks: *The bombs and skymines held in the racks of a Kharadron skyvessel can be swiftly deployed to stop enemy assaults in their tracks.*

At the start of the combat phase, you can pick 1 enemy unit within 1" of this model and roll a dice. On a 4+, that enemy unit suffers D3 mortal wounds.

Disengage: *Kharadron skyvessels can easily disengage from ground-based foes, flying away with all guns blazing.*

This model and any models in its garrison can retreat and still shoot in the same turn as long as there are no enemy units that can fly within 3" of this model at the start of the retreat move.

Fly High: *Kharadron skyvessels can swiftly soar up high in the air and then dive back down to the battlefield, ready to attack from a new direction.*

Instead of making a normal move with this model, you can say that it will fly high (it can retreat and disengage). If you do so, remove this model from the battlefield and set it up again more than 1" from any terrain features or objectives and more than 9" from any enemy models.

Drill Cannon: *The shells fired by a drill cannon burrow into the target and then explode, blasting shards of metal from the drill bit all around.*

If the unmodified hit roll for an attack made with a Drill Cannon is 5+, that attack inflicts 3 mortal wounds on the target and the attack sequence ends (do not make a wound or save roll).

Sky Cannon: *A sky cannon can either be loaded with shrapnel ammunition or an explosive shell.*

Before attacking with a Sky Cannon, choose either the Shrapnel or Shell missile weapon characteristics for that shooting attack.

KEYWORDS	ORDER, DUARDIN, KHARADRON OVERLORDS, WAR MACHINE, SKYVESSEL, GRUNDSTOK GUNHAULER

GRUNDSTOK THUNDERERS

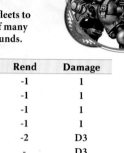

Grundstok Thunderers are heavily armoured marines employed by the airfleets to defend it from hostiles. Expert marksmen and battle-hardened veterans of many voyages, they obliterate their foes in a storm of aethershot and mortar rounds.

MISSILE WEAPONS	Range	Attacks	To Hit	To Wound	Rend	Damage
Aethershot Rifle	18"	2	3+	4+	-1	1
Double-barrelled Aethershot Rifle	18"	4	3+	4+	-1	1
Aetheric Fumigator	9"	3	3+	3+	-1	1
Decksweeper	12"	4	4+	4+	-1	1
Aethercannon	12"	1	4+	2+	-2	D3
Grundstok Mortar	12"	1	4+	3+	-	D3
MELEE WEAPONS	Range	Attacks	To Hit	To Wound	Rend	Damage
Drillbill	3"	D3	4+	4+	-1	1
Gun Butt	1"	1	4+	4+	-	1

MOVE 4"
WOUNDS 2
SAVE 4+
BRAVERY 7

DESCRIPTION

A unit of Grundstok Thunderers has any number of models, each armed with an Aethershot Rifle and Gun Butt. 1 in every 5 models can replace their Aethershot Rifle with a Grundstok Mortar. 1 in every 5 models can replace their Aethershot Rifle with an Aethercannon. 1 in every 5 models can replace their Aethershot Rifle with an Aetheric Fumigator. 1 in every 5 models can replace their Aethershot Rifle with a Decksweeper.

GUNNERY SERGEANT: 1 model in this unit can be a Gunnery Sergeant. Replace that model's weapons with a Double-barrelled Aethershot Rifle, Gun Butt and Drillbill.

HONOUR BEARER: 1 in every 5 models in this unit can be an Honour Bearer. You can re-roll battleshock tests for a unit that includes any Honour Bearers.

ABILITIES

Choking Fug: *Aetheric Fumigators fill the surrounding air with choking gas. The sealed suits worn by the Kharadron Overlords protect them from its effects, but this is not the case for their enemies…*

Subtract 1 from hit rolls for attacks made by enemy models within 3" of any friendly models armed with an Aetheric Fumigator. This ability cannot be used by a model that is part of a garrison.

Drive Them Back!: *Kharadron military history is filled with tales of Thunderers standing alone at battle's end surrounded by a circle of fallen foes.*

Add 1 to the Attacks characteristic of missile weapons used by this unit while any enemy units are within 3" of this unit. This ability cannot be used by a model that is part of a garrison.

Pin Them, Shred Them, Finish Them: *Thunderers use the specialist weapons they are armed with to launch a deadly combination of attacks that leaves the target reeling.*

Add 1 to hit rolls for attacks made with a Grundstok Mortar, Decksweeper or Aethercannon when it is used by a unit that has at least 1 of each of these weapons (i.e. at least 1 Grundstok Mortar, and at least 1 Decksweeper, and at least 1 Aethercannon). This ability cannot be used by a model that is part of a garrison.

KEYWORDS	ORDER, DUARDIN, KHARADRON OVERLORDS, SKYFARER, MARINE, GRUNDSTOK THUNDERERS

• WARSCROLL •

ENDRINRIGGERS

MOVE 12"
WOUNDS 2
SAVE 4+
BRAVERY 7

With aether-endrins strapped to their backs, Endrinriggers conduct repairs on their beloved airships miles above ground. In battle, their aether-powered tools become lethal weapons capable of punching through armour or messily sawing off limbs.

MISSILE WEAPONS	Range	Attacks	To Hit	To Wound	Rend	Damage
Aethermatic Volley Gun	24"	6	4+	4+	-1	1
Grapnel Launcher or Skyhook	24"	1	4+	3+	-2	3
Drill Launcher	24"	1	4+	3+	-3	D3
Rapid-fire Rivet Gun	12"	3	3+	4+	-1	1
MELEE WEAPONS	Range	Attacks	To Hit	To Wound	Rend	Damage
Aethermatic Saw	1"	1	3+	2+	-2	D3
Gun Butt	1"	1	4+	5+	-	1

DESCRIPTION

A unit of Endrinriggers has any number of models, each armed with a Rapid-fire Rivet Gun and Aethermatic Saw. 1 in every 3 models can replace their Rapid-fire Rivet Gun and Aethermatic Saw with an Aethermatic Volley Gun and Gun Butt. 1 in every 3 models can replace their Rapid-fire Rivet Gun and Aethermatic Saw with one of the following weapon options: Drill Launcher and Gun Butt; Grapnel Launcher and Gun Butt; or Skyhook and Gun Butt.

FLY: This unit can fly.

MIZZENMASTER: 1 model in this unit can be a Mizzenmaster. Add 1 to the Attacks characteristic of that model's melee weapons.

ABILITIES

Drill Launcher: *A handheld version of the drill cannons found aboard Kharadron gunships, the drill launcher fires a projectile that bores into its target before detonating.*

If the unmodified hit roll for an attack made with a Drill Launcher is 6, that attack inflicts 3 mortal wounds on the target and the attack sequence ends (do not make a wound or save roll).

Endrincraft: *Endrinriggers are expert mechanics, and keep all of the skyvessels in a Kharadron fleet shipshape.*

At the start of your hero phase, you can pick 1 friendly SKYVESSEL within 1" of this unit and roll 1 dice for each model in this unit. For each 4+, heal 1 wound allocated to that SKYVESSEL.

Grapnel Launcher: *Grapnel launchers are used to entangle the enemy and stop them from making their escape.*

Enemy units cannot retreat if they are within 3" of any models from this unit armed with a Grapnel Launcher.

Hitchers: *Kharadron kitted out with buoyancy endrins can attach themselves to a passing skyvessel and move alongside it.*

If this unit is wholly within 6" of a friendly SKYVESSEL immediately before the SKYVESSEL uses its Fly High ability, you can say that this unit will hitch a lift instead of making a normal move (as long as this unit has not already made a normal move in the same phase).

If you do so, after that SKYVESSEL has moved, remove this unit from the battlefield and set it up again wholly within 6" of that SKYVESSEL, more than 1" from any terrain features or objectives and more than 9" from any enemy models.

No more than 7 models can hitch a lift on the same SKYVESSEL in the same turn.

Skyhook: *Skyhooks are used to pull the bearer towards the foe.*

Add 1 to charge rolls for this unit if any models from this unit are armed with a Skyhook.

KEYWORDS	ORDER, DUARDIN, KHARADRON OVERLORDS, SKYFARERS, ENDRINRIGGERS

SKYWARDENS

MOVE 12"
WOUNDS 2
SAVE 4+
BRAVERY 7

Skywardens are elite formations of Arkanaut warriors granted the power of flight by portable aether-endrins. They swoop from on high to skewer enemies upon long-hafted skypikes or hover at short range to incinerate them with vulcaniser pistols.

MISSILE WEAPONS	Range	Attacks	To Hit	To Wound	Rend	Damage
Aethermatic Volley Gun	24"	6	4+	4+	-1	1
Grapnel Launcher or Skyhook	24"	1	4+	3+	-2	3
Drill Launcher	24"	1	4+	3+	-3	D3
Vulcaniser Pistol	9"	2	3+	3+	-1	1
MELEE WEAPONS	**Range**	**Attacks**	**To Hit**	**To Wound**	**Rend**	**Damage**
Skypike	2"	2	4+	3+	-1	D3
Gun Butt	1"	1	4+	5+	-	1

DESCRIPTION

A unit of Skywardens has any number of models, each armed with a Vulcaniser Pistol and Skypike. 1 in every 3 models can replace their Vulcaniser Pistol and Skypike with an Aethermatic Volley Gun and Gun Butt. 1 in every 3 models can replace their Vulcaniser Pistol and Skypike with one of the following weapon options: Drill Launcher and Gun Butt; Grapnel Launcher and Gun Butt; or Skyhook and Gun Butt.

FLY: This unit can fly.

CUSTODIAN: 1 model in this unit can be a Custodian. Add 1 to the Attacks characteristic of that model's melee weapons.

ABILITIES

Drill Launcher: *A handheld version of the drill cannons found aboard Kharadron gunships, the drill launcher fires a projectile that bores into its target before detonating.*

If the unmodified hit roll for an attack made with a Drill Launcher is 6, that attack inflicts 3 mortal wounds on the target and the attack sequence ends (do not make a wound or save roll).

Grapnel Launcher: *Grapnel launchers are used to entangle the enemy and stop them from making their escape.*

Enemy units cannot retreat if they are within 3" of any models from this unit armed with a Grapnel Launcher.

Hitchers: *Kharadron kitted out with buoyancy endrins can attach themselves to a passing skyvessel and move alongside it.*

If this unit is wholly within 6" of a friendly **SKYVESSEL** immediately before the **SKYVESSEL** uses its Fly High ability, you can say that this unit will hitch a lift instead of making a normal move (as long as this unit has not already made a normal move in the same phase).

If you do so, after that **SKYVESSEL** has moved, remove this unit from the battlefield and set it up again wholly within 6" of that **SKYVESSEL**, more than 1" from any terrain features or objectives and more than 9" from any enemy models.

No more than 7 models can hitch a lift on the same **SKYVESSEL** in the same turn.

Skyhook: *Skyhooks are used to pull the bearer towards the foe.*

Add 1 to charge rolls for this unit if any models from this unit are armed with a Skyhook.

Skymines: *Skywardens surround themselves with airborne mines that explode on contact.*

If an enemy unit that can fly ends a charge move within 1" of any friendly units with this ability, you can roll 1 dice for each model in that enemy unit. For each 6, that unit suffers 1 mortal wound.

Timed Charges: *Skywardens are practised at striking hard and then retreating quickly amidst timed explosions to cause massive damage.*

Roll 1 dice for each enemy unit that is within 3" of this unit immediately before this unit makes a retreat move. On a 4+, the unit being rolled for suffers D3 mortal wounds.

KEYWORDS | ORDER, DUARDIN, KHARADRON OVERLORDS, SKYFARERS, SKYWARDENS

PITCHED BATTLE PROFILES

The table below provides points, minimum unit sizes and battlefield roles for the warscrolls and warscroll battalions in this book, for use in Pitched Battles. Spending the points listed on this table allows you to take a minimum-sized unit with any of its upgrades. Understrength units cost the full amount of points. Larger units are taken in multiples of their minimum unit size; multiply their cost by the same amount as you multiplied their size. If a unit has two points values separated by a slash (e.g. '60/200'), the second value is for a maximum-sized unit. Units that are listed as 'Unique' are named characters and can only be taken once in an army. A unit that has any of the keywords listed on the Allies table can be taken as an allied unit by a Kharadron Overlords army. Updated January 2020; the profiles printed here take precedence over any profiles with an earlier publication date or no publication date.

KHARADRON OVERLORDS WARSCROLL	UNIT SIZE MIN	UNIT SIZE MAX	POINTS	BATTLEFIELD ROLE	NOTES
Arkanaut Company	10	40	90	Battleline	
Arkanaut Frigate	1	1	250	Behemoth	Battleline if **BARAK-ZILFIN**
Arkanaut Ironclad	1	1	510	Behemoth	
Aether-Khemist	1	1	90	Leader	
Aetheric Navigator	1	1	100	Leader	
Arkanaut Admiral	1	1	140	Leader	
Brokk Grungsson, Lord-Magnate of Barak-Nar	1	1	240	Leader	Unique
Endrinmaster with Dirigible Suit	1	1	220	Leader	
Endrinmaster with Endrinharness	1	1	100	Leader	
Bjorgen Thundrik	1	1	140	Leader	Unique. These units must be taken as a set for a total of 140 points. Although taken as a set, each is a separate unit.
Thundrik's Profiteers	4	4			
Endrinriggers	3	12	100		Battleline if general is Endrinmaster with Dirigible Suit
Grundstok Gunhauler	1	1	150		Battleline if **BARAK-URBAZ**
Grundstok Thunderers	5	20	120		Battleline if **BARAK-NAR**
Skywardens	3	12	100		Battleline if general is Endrinmaster with Dirigible Suit
Grand Armada	-	-	90	Warscroll Battalion	
Grundstok Escort Wing	-	-	140	Warscroll Battalion	
Iron Sky Attack Squadron	-	-	120	Warscroll Battalion	
Iron Sky Command	-	-	130	Warscroll Battalion	

FACTION	ALLIES
Kharadron Overlords	Dispossessed, Fyreslayers, Ironweld Arsenal, Stormcast Eternal